#WHATIS

#WHATIS
POST-TRAUMATIC
GROWTH?

The Journey from Adversity to Growth

MIRIAM AKHTAR

This edition first published in the UK and USA 2017 by
Watkins, an imprint of Watkins Media Limited
19 Cecil Court
London WC2N 4EZ

enquiries@watkinspublishing.com

1 3 5 7 9 10 8 6 4 2

Designed and typeset by Manisha Patel

Printed and bound in Germany

A CIP record for this book is available from the British Library

ISBN: 978-1-78028-979-3

www.watkinspublishing.com

CONTENTS

Why read this book?

Sometimes in life an event shakes us to the core. It could be a sudden death or the shock of a diagnosis of terminal illness. It could be something outside normal experience, like being caught in an earthquake, or a common but no less traumatic development such as a divorce. Such things have a huge impact, sending out shockwaves that can rock every corner of our world. They can leave us feeling lost, overwhelmed and vulnerable. The good news is that this doesn't have to define us. In fact it can herald a new beginning.

'Post-traumatic stress' (PTS) is something that we hear about a lot, for example among survivors of 9/11 and soldiers who served in Iraq and Afghanistan. The coverage has led to a growing awareness of the far-reaching effects of trauma and 'post-traumatic stress disorder', known as PTSD. This was first identified in military veterans (see page 42) but we are coming to understand that it is experienced more widely.

Although most of us will have to deal with extreme stresses at some point in life, these don't have to condemn us to eternal suffering. There can be a way ahead. If you have picked up this book because you think you, or someone you know, may be suffering from post-traumatic stress, I hope you will find it comforting to hear that something more positive may also be taking place: something that will allow us to experience positive change as a consequence of trauma. This is post-traumatic growth (PTG).

My intention in writing this book is to provide you with an introductory guide to trauma, PTS and PTG. We can't deny that traumatic experiences are both difficult and life-altering, but they can also be the catalyst for personal growth. My wish is to show that there can be a silver lining to trauma and that it can bring about a positive transformation.

20 reasons to start reading

1   Understand the nature of trauma.
2   Recognize the signs of post-traumatic stress (PTS).
3   Understand the difference between PTS and PTSD.
4   Discover the three major changes that happen with PTG.
5   Get to know the five dimensions of PTG.
6   Understand how PTG can change life for the better.
7   Learn from the stories of people who've experienced PTG.
8   Draw on modern science to support the healing process.
9   Understand the body–mind connection in trauma.
10 Practise self-care while going through extreme stress.
11 Strengthen your resilience to cope with challenges.
12 Use positive psychology to rebuild your well-being.
13 Be better equipped to support a loved one through trauma.
14 Understand how people grow through adversity.
15 Adopt a 'growth mindset' to lay the foundations for PTG.

16 Discover a new sense of meaning and purpose.

17 Explore five pathways to PTG.

18 Experience the deeper form of happiness known as 'eudaimonic well-being' (see pages 133–135).

19 Feel encouraged to embark on a fresh chapter in life.

20 Apply new knowledge to move from surviving toward thriving.

This book aims to point you to the tools that can help you reach the light at the end of the tunnel. It is possible to emerge stronger from the most testing of times and PTG can take you toward a life of greater meaning and deeper happiness.

Key features of this book

This book combines the science of PTG with real-life stories of people experiencing it. Apart from a few exceptions, all names have been changed to preserve the anonymity of the people who shared their stories.

In the Introduction I explain how I came to have an interest in post-traumatic growth through my work and my own personal experience. Chapter 1 explains the characteristics of trauma and how to recognize the symptoms of post-traumatic stress. Chapter 2 outlines the five key features of PTG and three ways in which it can change our lives. Chapter 3 focuses on the body and self-care while Chapter 4 looks at the mind and resilience. Finally Chapter 5 explores the transformative process of PTG and its impact on spiritual well-being.

The book is designed to make PTG as accessible as possible with the help of the following features:

- A Q&A approach that, chapter by chapter, explores the questions that are often asked about PTG.
- 'Case Study' boxes that share real-life experiences of PTG.
- 'Focus On' boxes that explore particular elements of PTG and therapies that can help achieve this.
- 'Try It' boxes that give you practical exercises to try out to help you on the road from adversity to growth.
- Finally, a 'What Next' section, including a further reading list, suggests how to continue your exploration of PTG.

KEY ABBREVIATIONS

The following abbreviations are used throughout the book for key terms:

PTG – Post-traumatic growth
PTS – Post-traumatic stress
PTSD – Post-traumatic stress disorder

INTRODUCTION

Why this subject?

Most of us will suffer trauma at some point in our lives. It's part of being human. When we do hit a major crisis, the extreme stress can shatter our emotional well-being and overwhelm our ability to cope. Trauma disrupts our lives, yet it used to be that people were expected to keep a lid on their emotions and just 'get on with it'. It was a taboo subject and people were often left in despair, silently tormented by distressing symptoms such as flashbacks which could go on for years.

This book intends to challenge those taboos about post-traumatic stress, making it clear that PTS is a normal, natural response to abnormal events. There's nothing to feel guilty or ashamed about.

Awareness of post-traumatic stress disorder has grown greatly, largely due to the increasing numbers being diagnosed with it. However, PTSD still tends to be associated with events outside normal experience, such as acts of war or terrorism. This very limited take on trauma urgently needs upgrading for the 21st century as it's not so much what happens that determines whether an event is traumatic, but our subjective emotional experience of it. The truth is that the more vulnerable and helpless we feel, the more likely we are to be traumatized by all kinds of unexpected negative events, whether that's being the victim of an assault, suffering a major financial loss or facing relentless stresses from working in a toxic environment. As we search for ways to deal with the crisis, we may question all aspects of our lives as we try to make sense of the adversity.

People sometimes find it hard to recognize that they are suffering from PTS and therefore often lack the tools to help themselves. The purpose of this book is to offer a way *through* trauma. There is an urgent need for a more positive approach to give people hope in the bleakest of times and the confidence that something good can emerge from the suffering. 'I no longer see what life took from me – I see what it gave me,' says Tara Lal, a firefighter, whose story is one of the case studies in this book.

Why me?

I first came across PTG during my training in positive psychology, which is the study of optimal human functioning – what it takes to feel good and function well. One of positive psychology's concepts is of people growing through adversity. This intrigued me as I had experienced this process myself. The trauma of losing my father when I was young shaped the course of my life. I learnt that life is short and that i had to apply myself to make the most of it. When you've been through the worst thing possible, nothing else ever seems as bad or as difficult to cope with.

The loss did, however, sow the seeds for later episodes of depression, and it was through the search for a solution that I discovered positive psychology. To my relief, I found the scientifically grounded tools that helped me develop a more sustainable happiness. I went on to become one of the first people in the UK to qualify as a positive psychologist, in 2009, gaining the MAPP – the MSc in Applied Positive Psychology. This course was established by Prof. Martin Seligman, the co-founder of the field, at the University of Pennsylvania, 'to make the world a happier place, parallel to the way clinical psychologists have made the world a less unhappy place.'

As soon as I qualified I began working with people to help them flourish in their personal and professional lives. And today I still work one-to-one as a coach as well as designing well-being programmes that range from Positive Youth to Positive Ageing, all work that I find hugely meaningful.

Mental health is one of my areas of expertise and in 2012 I wrote the book *Positive Psychology for Overcoming Depression*, which was a ground-breaking departure from the traditional approach to depression. The book has now been published around the world and I love hearing from readers who have been helped by it. It's made me aware of how useful self-help books can be to sustain people through their dark night of the soul.

Life sometimes throws a curveball at you and a few years ago, in the space of one month, I suffered a double trauma. Out of the blue I became the target of a very modern crime – cyberstalking – and hard on its heels came another experience, which brought back all the distress of my childhood loss. My mother collapsed and was taken into intensive care at the hospital where my father had died. I was at a conference in Amsterdam and my emergency flight home was delayed. I paced around the airport, desperate to get to my mother's bedside in time. When I got to the hospital I found myself walking down the very corridor where 40 years earlier I had witnessed my father's face contorting as his heart arrested. I was taken into a private room where a doctor told me that my mother had less than a 40 per cent chance of survival. One of these crises might have severely tested my resilience, but having two to deal with crushed me. After months of turmoil I was eventually diagnosed with PTSD.

My turning point came on the day I was confiding in a friend about the cyberstalking. She looked at me and said: 'Miriam, you can do something with this. You can use this experience to help others in the future.' And that's how I began to shift out of the grip of fear and into a place of motivation. I realized that I could help myself and others going through a similar experience. My journalistic skills resurfaced and I began to explore the practices that you'll find in this book.

At the core of this book are techniques that build resilience. I train frontline medics in resilience skills and have facilitated one of the major courses in the field, the Penn Resilience Programme. Originally developed at the University of Pennsylvania to support adolescent well-being, it is now being delivered at an adult level across the American military, from where a lot of the research on PTG has emerged.

I have given talks on resilience at various conferences and healthcare facilities including the Bristol Cancer Help Centre, now known as Penny Brohn UK, a charity that is a pioneer of complementary cancer care. I've seen people after the trauma of their cancer diagnosis expressing a desperate need for ways to help themselves. I have also had the privilege of seeing how people go on to grow despite dealing with life-threatening illness. They know what's important and who's important to them.

There's no doubt that trauma can be an enfeebling experience when you're in the thick of it, yet I now feel stronger than I did before. My hope is that this book will help to strengthen you too.

Why now?

The concept of growing through adversity is not a new one. 'That which does not kill us makes us stronger' is a well-known saying attributed to the philosopher Friedrich Nietzsche. The phoenix rising from the ashes is a long-established symbol of rebirth that is highly relevant to PTG. At the end of the phoenix's long life its nest catches fire and burns ferociously, reducing the bird to ashes. But out of those ashes a young phoenix emerges – renewed and stronger than before: the perfect symbol of regeneration after a life-altering event.

Many ancient forms of spirituality, including Christianity, Buddhism and Judaism, speak of the transformative power of suffering. What is new is that there is now a *science* of PTG. Studies by the Posttraumatic Growth Research Group at the University of North Carolina, the Post-Traumatic Growth Unit at the University of East London and the Centre for Trauma, Resilience and Growth at the University of Nottingham have all confirmed that people can and do experience benefits from adversity.

With mental health disorders on the rise in our fast-moving, increasingly pressured world, there is a grave need for greater choice in treatment methods. As help is often hard to access through health services or expensive to fund yourself, the knowledge in this book gives you self-help tools to cope positively in stressful circumstances, stand firm while the storm rages around you and make the longed-for journey toward a renewed and flourishing life.

CHAPTER 1
What is trauma? And what
is post-traumatic stress?

Experiencing the dark side of life, such as the sudden death of a loved one, the shock of a diagnosis of illness or the end of a significant relationship, are all normal parts of being human. If we look back over the generations of our parents and grandparents, there are many examples of hardship and horrors, everything from deprivation to war. Trauma is an experience of the brain and body in reaction to conditions of great stress. Mostly we do find the courage and strength to adapt to events that take us to our limits. The spirit is surprisingly hardy and can recover from testing experiences.

How do we experience stress?

The stress response is at the core of a traumatic experience. Stress is the body's way of responding to any kind of demand and reacting to what it perceives as threatening situations – whether those are real or imagined. In physiological terms stress releases hormones that prepare us for 'fight or flight', gearing us up to take action. Feeling 'stressed' has come to be a defining feature of modern life, whether that is dealing with job insecurity or juggling work/life balance. While we tend to think of stress as generally a negative thing, it does have an upside. A little stress can motivate us to get started on a project and a deadline can help sharpen our focus.

Being exposed to stressful situations on an intermittent basis can even serve to strengthen us so that we're better

FOCUS ON THE 'FIGHT OR FLIGHT' RESPONSE

The autonomic nervous system, which regulates our internal organs, has two main branches:

- The parasympathetic nervous system (PNS) – the branch that helps us to 'rest and digest', taking us into a state of calm and relaxation.
- The sympathetic nervous system (SNS) – the branch that produces the stress response, aka 'fight or flight', which primes the body to defend itself against threat, an essential part of our survival mechanism.

When the SNS is in control, stress hormones such as cortisol and adrenaline are released, the heart rate increases, blood pressure rises, breathing accelerates and muscles tighten, ready for action. Traumatic stress is associated with being in constant 'fight or flight' mode – or its cousin the 'freeze', when we switch off and become numb in response to overwhelming events. A heightened state of the SNS, known as 'hyper-arousal', is an indicator that the body and mind have not yet recognized when a traumatic event is over. This state of increased psychological and physiological tension is one of the main symptoms of PTSD.

prepared for future stressors, like a form of 'stress inoculation'. However, prolonged stress, when life is continuously out of balance, can compromise our psychological, emotional and physical well-being. The question is, therefore, where does stress cross the line into something else? And at what point does stress turn into trauma?

How do people respond to major stress?

When people are faced with an extremely stressful event, there are three main ways in which they may respond. To use a real-life example, as I write this, floods have struck the south-west of England, close to where I live. In rural Somerset villages are under water and homes are drowning in thick, smelly mud. Roads have become rivers, communities are cut off from the outside world and businesses are in danger of collapse. When an emergency such as this happens, people may experience:

- A sense of being overwhelmed and traumatized with a lasting effect of it overshadowing their lives.
- Stress and strain for a time but then go on to make a recovery back to how they were before.
- A sense of positive change as a consequence of going through the adversity with surprising bonuses such as stronger friendships and community spirit, with people pulling together and looking out for each other.

The lesson in this is that it is not the event in itself that creates a 'trauma' but rather people's perception of what has happened to them. This is important because, as we'll find out later, only one person can say whether an experience was traumatic, and that is the individual going through it.

What is really meant by 'trauma'?

'Trauma' is a word that comes from the Greek for 'wound' and in the medical sense refers to a physical injury. In psychology it's a term used to describe highly distressing events that have the power to overwhelm. Traumatic experiences are often unexpected and uncontrollable occurrences that people feel unprepared for and powerless to prevent. They provoke intense fear, horror and a feeling of helplessness. Trauma poses a significant threat to our psychological and physical well-being. It often involves life-and-death scenarios that happen to us or that we witness in others. A traumatizing experience shakes the foundations of our beliefs about safety and shatters our trust in life. It causes emotional, psychological and physical harm, which can seriously disrupt the course of our lives.

How do you know when you're experiencing trauma?

Historically, and often still today, we tend to think of traumatic events as horrendous one-off incidents, like being the victim of an assault or caught up in an act of terrorism, but they

CASESTUDY SURVIVING A TSUNAMI

This trauma survivor was caught up in the 2004 Indian Ocean tsunami. 'My partner and I were on a beautiful beach in Thailand when the tsunami struck. Having stepped inside a bamboo hut just seconds before, I quickly, and terrifyingly, became submerged as the water crashed in. I was thrown around underwater like a ragdoll and smashed several times against the back wall, but then somehow I surfaced outside the hut, presumably after a second wave had knocked down some of the walls. I then swam as hard as I could but I was being pulled out to sea when a Thai man appeared in a tree and somehow – to this day I still don't know how – managed to pull me into it, to safety.

It was only later after we swam to dry land that I was lucky enough to find my partner, who had been separated from me in the chaos. He was in a bad way by this stage due to his injuries. Several days later we made it to a hospital in Bangkok, where his head wound was addressed and his leg was saved.'

Find out how our trauma survivor coped in the aftermath of the tsunami on page 29.

can also involve lower-level repeated incidents. This book is using a wider definition of trauma to include chronic, insidious experiences such as the coercive control involved in abusive relationships, where the relentlessness and stress of the situation can trigger a traumatic reaction. The circumstances may include a betrayal of trust, abuse of power, pain, confusion, entrapment, loss or other negative experiences.

What makes something a traumatic experience?

Whether someone is traumatized by what has happened will depend on a wide range of circumstances including their:

CASESTUDY **AUTHOR IS CYBERSTALKED**

'One day out of the blue I was contacted by a client, who was perplexed by a malicious email they'd received about me. I was shocked and embarrassed. As I looked into it I discovered that the culprit was posting lies online while at the same time trying to impersonate my business. I felt wave after wave of horror as I uncovered the scale of his campaign of cyber harassment. It was the obsessiveness of it that was most frightening. It was like he was trying to destroy me and I felt powerless to stop him.'

- **subjective experience** of the event – e.g. when someone in an accident *believes* they are going to die.
- **personal circumstances,** including any other pressures they are under and if they have recently suffered other traumas.
- **physical health,** whether they're in good health or more vulnerable as a result of illness.
- **mental health,** including coping skills and resilience levels.
- **support** that they have around them at the time of the incident.

No two people's experience will ever be the same. Whether it is a one-off incident that leaves you in a state of helplessness and hopelessness or the reaction to a prolonged stress that eats away at your resilience, it's up to you to decide if it has been a traumatic experience.

What kind of experiences can trigger a trauma?

In the list below I've included some of the more common events that can lead to a traumatic reaction as well as a broad range of others. However, it's important to remember that absolutely any distressing occurrence or situation has the potential to be traumatic, whether you experienced it directly or witnessed it.

- Accidents
- Bullying
- Child abuse or neglect
- Crime

- Cyber harassment
- Death, especially a sudden death or suicide
- Discrimination
- Divorce
- Domestic violence
- Emotional abuse
- Entrapment
- Financial crisis or loss
- Harassment
- Homelessness
- Incarceration
- Maltreatment or neglect
- Man-made disasters e.g. chemical spills, nuclear accidents
- Military combat and service
- Natural disasters e.g. floods, earthquakes, volcanic eruptions
- Racism
- Rape
- Relationship breakdown
- Scapegoating or shunning
- Serious illness
- Sexual abuse or assault
- Stalking
- Surgery
- Terrorism
- Toxic workplaces
- Traumatic birth
- Traumatic separation

This list doesn't cover every possibility so I recommend also taking a look at the symptoms that are listed on pages 30–33 to help you evaluate your own particular experience and identify whether or not you've been suffering from post-traumatic stress.

People react in very different ways to trauma, making it hard to predict how symptoms will manifest and across what timeframe. Shock, denial and emotional numbing are common immediately after a horrific incident as people find it hard to comprehend and adjust to the new reality. The reaction can come in waves and reappear after a period of absence. A trauma can also catch you by surprise by revisiting you at later points in life, in particular at times when you are vulnerable for other reasons. Trauma often involves a sense of loss, whether of a loved one, the life you were living, a job, home or relationship and, at a fundamental level, it represents a loss of your sense of safety in life. As such, it is normal to go through a grieving process following the traumatic event.

What is post-traumatic stress (PTS)?

PTS is a normal stress reaction that follows on from a traumatic event, which appears as any of a wide range of emotional, behavioural, physical and social symptoms (see the lists on pages 30–33) that occur as the mind slips into a state of overwhelm and the body into fight, flight or freeze mode. The key to understanding PTS is recognizing that what is going on is a natural, and indeed helpful, response to what is perceived as a dangerous situation.

In my own experience of PTS, one of the most difficult aspects was the insomnia. I'd pace around at night and go to the window to check and see if my cyberstalker was there. My face was red and raw, covered in patches of eczema.

I couldn't concentrate and was in such a state that I was unable to work. I stopped going out at night and would get panicky about going up to London to see clients. Some of my fillings fell out because I was grinding my teeth. I felt like I was imploding, swinging between periods of high anxiety and then feeling so low that I was barely able to function.

CASESTUDY **AFTER THE TSUNAMI**

The journey to recovery was not straightforward for the tsunami survivor we met on page 24. 'It was the body and mind's amazing instinct for survival which got me through early on. Back in the UK, my partner suffered badly from depression while I, on the other hand, felt strong, feeling lucky just to be alive and to have the support of so many friends and family. However, about a year later, as he was starting to recover, I began to feel disproportionately overwhelmed by things and then, one day, I couldn't get out of bed. My back had gone and I just lay there crying, not really knowing why. I found it hard to function on a day-to-day level, as everything felt so heavy and difficult. I was checked over by various specialists, and the consensus was that I was suffering from classic PTS symptoms.'

How do you recognize the signs of PTS or PTSD?

Although trauma is a unique experience for each individual, there are common features to traumatic stress. Whether you are suffering from PTS or the more extreme PTSD, it is likely that you will relate to some of the physical, emotional, behavioural and social symptoms described in the lists that follow, which have been sourced primarily from mental health and medical guides including MIND, HelpGuide and Web-MD (please see the Further Reading and Useful Websites sections, pages 138–141, for details of these and others). In real life there is considerable overlap between the symptoms of PTS, which is a normal stress reaction, and PTSD, which is considered to be a medical disorder. For that reason I've made the list inclusive of both. There are, however, particular criteria for a diagnosis of PTSD (see pages 35–37).

Physical symptoms

Let's start with the physical symptoms of trauma. The body is in a state of heightened physiological stress, signs of which include being easily startled and finding it hard to fall asleep. You may also feel extremely tired due to sleep disturbances and peaks and troughs of stress hormones like adrenaline and cortisol. Physical symptoms include the following:

- Racing heart
- Muscle tension
- Excessive startle response
- Shaky hands

- Insomnia
- Bad dreams
- Fatigue
- Headaches
- Lowered immune functioning
- Digestive upsets and problems
- Aches and pains
- Loss of appetite
- Lower libido

Emotional symptoms

A feeling of helplessness and hopelessness are both common features of PTS, as are a variety of negative emotions, from being held in the grip of fear to feeling weighed down with sadness. 'Survivor's guilt' is another common experience for victims of incidents in which others have died. Often people swing between highs and lows. Positive emotions are largely absent, although this is not a black and white scenario. It is entirely possible and indeed human to experience both positive and negative emotions at the same time – moments of joy tinged with sadness, for example.

Behavioural symptoms

A trauma can impact on how well you function and your behaviour in everyday life. Hypervigilance is common in PTS, repeatedly scanning your environment for anything that feels threatening or may be linked to the trauma. This can lead to some obsessive behaviour patterns. Behavioural PTS symptoms include:

- Extreme alertness, on the lookout for signs of danger
- Agitation
- Avoidance of places associated with the trauma
- Confusion and disorientation
- Detachment
- Disassociation
- Disbelief and denial of the events
- Poor concentration
- Intrusive thoughts and memories
- Difficulty with decision-making
- Memory problems
- Loss of confidence and self-esteem
- Loss of interest in usual activities
- Self-blame

Social symptoms

As well as wrecking our inner world, the ripples of trauma often disrupt our relationships, damage how we interact with others in daily life, and undermine our trust in the world. So look out for signs such as:

- A sense of alienation, rejection or abandonment
- Major conflict in relationships
- Blaming and distrust of others
- Vulnerability around people
- Social withdrawal and isolation

- Lower performance at work
- Overprotectiveness
- Reduced satisfaction with the world

PTS triggers

It's very common to have an acute stress reaction following a traumatic experience but PTS symptoms will usually subside as the trauma is processed.

However, even when recovered, it is possible to be troubled from time to time by painful memories or emotions, and for these to be triggered via the senses. Shooting survivors, for example, are often set off by sounds that resemble gunfire. 'The thing that gets me tearful is bottles of champagne popping. Balloons and fireworks are a big fear, and party poppers. I really don't like those,' says Aimie Adam, who, as a child, survived the 1996 Dunblane school massacre.

A female client of mine, who was a victim of sexual abuse, is triggered by seeing a certain make of car which was driven by the perpetrator. Her other senses can provoke a similar reaction too: 'Smelling a certain aftershave also makes me collapse for a few seconds. I just wake up on the floor.' Anniversaries, certain places or situations or even news items related to your trauma can be the triggers that plunge you straight back into full-scale distress.

Usually, with time and self-care, the symptoms of PTS will improve, but if they worsen or continue for months and interfere with your functioning, then it is important to see your doctor or another health professional with expertise in the area as there is a possibility that you may be suffering from the more serious post-traumatic stress disorder (PTSD).

What is PTSD?

It may surprise you to learn that the most common outcome following high adversity is NOT post-traumatic stress disorder (PTSD) but rather resilience, returning to your previous level of functioning after a short period of suffering. PTSD, on the other hand, is a complex and debilitating psychiatric disorder, in which symptoms such as flashbacks can persist for months and years after the adversity. Similarly PTSD symptoms can also emerge a long time after the traumatizing event.

The American Psychiatric Association classifies PTSD as a trauma- and stress-related disorder that can arise from exposure to actual or threatened death, serious injury or sexual violation. Their criteria for a diagnosis of PTSD are specific. The exposure is as a result of one of the following scenarios:

- Directly experiencing the traumatic event
- Witnessing the traumatic event in person

- Learning that the traumatic event occurred to a close family member or good friend (with the actual or threatened death being either violent or accidental)
- Experiencing first-hand repeated or extreme exposure to aversive details of the traumatic event

How is PTSD diagnosed?

PTSD is usually diagnosed when, more than a month after the traumatic event, symptoms are continuing to cause significant distress or disturbance, interfering with home, work, relationships or other important areas of functioning. According to the *Diagnostic and Statistical Manual of Mental Disorders* (*DSM-5*; the standard classification used by mental health professionals in the USA), an individual will have symptoms from each of four clusters for a diagnosis of PTSD:

- **Re-experiencing the trauma.** Flashbacks, memories or dreams, as well as intense distress in response to cues that represent some aspect of the traumatic event.
- **Hyperarousal.** A state of heightened physiological and psychological stress which can result in anxiety, fatigue and reduced tolerance to pain. An exaggerated startle response is a classic sign of hyperarousal, as is insomnia. It also often causes problems with concentration as well as anger, aggression, agitation, impulsiveness, irritability and reckless and self-destructive behaviour.

- **Avoidance of anything associated with the trauma.** This includes efforts to avoid memories, thoughts and feelings as well as external reminders – people, places, activities and situations that are linked to the event.
- **Negative alterations in thinking and mood.** Persistent and exaggerated negative thoughts, beliefs and emotions toward yourself and others, e.g. blaming yourself for what happened and feeling incapable of experiencing positive emotions.

There is also a dissociative subtype of PTSD. Someone experiencing this is likely to feel entirely detached from their life, as if:

- they are an outside observer of their own mind and body
- they or their world is not real
- they are in a dreamlike state

Women are more than twice as likely as men to develop post-traumatic stress disorder, according to the National Center for PTSD in the USA. It's suggested that around 10 per cent of women in the USA will experience PTSD at some point in their lives compared to 4 per cent of men. Amongst the emergency services, 20 per cent of firefighters are estimated to experience PTSD. The incidence is also high amongst military personnel, estimated at 11–20 per cent of veterans.

There are some gender differences in the experience of PTSD. Sexual assault and abuse are the major causes in women, whereas in men there are more diverse causes including accidents, physical assault, combat and disasters, and indirect causes such as witnessing death or injury. Depression, substance abuse and anxiety disorders frequently co-occur with PTSD. Women tend to experience 'internalizing' disorders such as depression and anxiety whereas with men it often

FOCUS ON UNDERSTANDING PTSD FLASHBACKS

Some experts prefer to think of PTSD as a psychological injury rather than a mental disorder. The brain suffers what is in essence a 'memory-filing error' when trying to process the trauma. This can be very distressing as the brain is unable to recognize the event as a normal 'memory' because it wasn't processed as one. All the elements of the trauma – the event itself, the emotions involved, together with sensations such as sights, sounds and smells – can end up being presented in the form of flashbacks, as if they are happening again. Such flashbacks cause an individual to be sent straight back into their trauma and feel as if they are re-experiencing it in the here and now.

manifests in externalizing symptoms such as rage, aggressive behaviour and substance misuse.

People most at risk of PTSD include those who have been exposed to life-and-death scenarios as witnesses, rescuers or supporters, or the perpetrators themselves. Trauma impacts on a wide range of first responders and other personnel who assist trauma survivors, such as social workers, therapists, health professionals and clergy. This is known as vicarious traumatization.

Are PTS and PTSD the same thing?

In everyday language PTS and PTSD are terms that are used interchangeably, although as we have seen there are specific criteria for a clinical diagnosis of PTSD. Many of the symptoms in PTSD are similar to PTS but the difference lies in the duration and intensity of symptoms. Dr Matthew Friedman, senior advisor to the American National Center for PTSD, likens it to the difference between a cold and pneumonia. They share many symptoms, but if your cold is extremely severe and hasn't gone away in more than a week, something more is at work and you should get it checked out. I find it helpful to think of a continuum with PTS at the milder end where the body and mind eventually succeed in consigning the trauma to the past. At the other end is the medical disorder of PTSD where problems processing the trauma mean

that it continues to haunt the survivor in the present, and
professional support should be sought.

Unfortunately many people suffer in silence, whether out of
a sense of shame or simply not knowing what to do, which

FOCUSON **DIFFERENCES BETWEEN PTS AND PTSD**

PTS	PTSD
A traumatic experience that overwhelms the sufferer's ability to cope for a finite time	Experiencing or witnessing a life-threatening event that causes significant distress and disturbance
A normal stress response to a trauma	Clinically diagnosed psychiatric disorder
Symptoms usually last less than one month	Symptoms continue for more than one month or emerge later
Symptoms are intense at first but eventually subside	Symptoms are severe, persistent and can reoccur
Temporarily interferes with daily life	Has a significant and lasting impact on functioning

---

means that they can end up falling between the cracks, neither recognizing what is ailing them nor getting access to help. There is one clear advantage of being given a professional diagnosis of PTSD and that is that it opens up a potential pathway to treatment.

What is the history of PTSD?

Humans have always been exposed to trauma but in the past the symptoms that ensued were often put down to a weakness of character or body rather than a wound to the psyche. As early as the 17th century Swiss military physicians identified a condition they named 'nostalgia', which was characterized by melancholy, incessant thinking about home, disturbed sleep, loss of appetite, anxiety and cardiac palpitations. Other nationalities began to recognize the symptoms. The Germans called it *heimweh* or homesickness, while French doctors similarly named it *maladie du pays* and the Spanish *estar roto* – to be broken. This was a condition most often observed in soldiers but in civilian life there were also signs of the symptoms which would come to be associated with PTSD.

It was through the experience of war that PTSD eventually came to be identified but it took a long time to recognize that injuries sustained in war were psychological as well as physical. In the early 20th century, soldiers returning from the

CASE STUDY CHARLES DICKENS, A PTSD VICTIM?

In 1865 the novelist Charles Dickens had a brush with death when he was a passenger on a train which plunged off a viaduct into a river below. It took several hours for rescuers to arrive so Dickens worked amongst the dead and dying, witnessing trauma as well as suffering it himself. He later wrote about feeling 'curiously weak . . . and very nervous'. Dickens subsequently avoided travelling by train, finding it 'inexpressibly distressing'. At the time, rail accident victims without apparent physical wounds were found to be experiencing debilitating nerve problems such as trembling, exhaustion and chronic pain. This condition became known as 'railway spine' and was formally named 'Erichsen's disease' after the physician John Eric Erichsen, who described it in his 1866 publication: *On Railway and Other Injuries of the Nervous System*. Symptoms included memory impairment, poor concentration, sleep disturbance, anxiety, irritability, back stiffness and pain, hearing problems, numbness of extremities and head, hand and arm pain. Dickens's output dwindled after the crash and, in a strange coincidence, he died on its fifth anniversary. Maybe he was suffering from what we now know to be PTSD.

battlefields of World War One were observed suffering major anxiety, panic, agitation, helplessness, extreme sensitivity to noise and other symptoms of what we now know as PTSD. It was named 'shell shock' and thought to be caused by the impact on the brain of artillery shell explosions. Tragically this condition was little understood and sufferers were sometimes put on trial, and even executed, for military crimes such as desertion and cowardice.

Thinking began to change when soldiers who had not been in the line of fire were also found to be suffering from symptoms. Men were breaking down, unable to cope with the stresses of warfare. An inability to eat or sleep was common. A German doctor called Honigman came up with 'war neurosis' as a term to describe the multitude of nervous and mental disorders associated with military combat. Sigmund Freud, the founder of psychoanalysis, became involved in the diagnosis and treatment of this 'war neurosis'.

Through the course of subsequent wars the understanding of the condition evolved. The plight of American veterans of the Vietnam War, together with an emerging field of study on trauma, was the turning point that led to the modern definition of PTSD. In 1980 it made its first appearance in the third edition of the *Diagnostic and Statistical Manual*. The term 'post-traumatic stress disorder' (PTSD) was chosen to reflect the fact that the condition isn't only a phenomenon of war but had also been observed in victims of the Nazi Holocaust, the atomic bombings of Hiroshima and Nagasaki, and other traumas including torture, rape, natural disasters such as earthquakes, and man-made disasters such as factory explosions. The crucial change was the stipulation that the cause of PTSD lay outside the individual – it was a result of a traumatic event rather than an inherent personal weakness.

The criteria for a diagnosis of PTSD have broadened across subsequent editions of the *DSM*. The International Classification of Diseases (ICD) developed by the World Health Organization states that the PTSD patient 'must have been exposed to a stressful event or situation (either short or long-lasting) of an exceptionally threatening or catastrophic nature, which would be likely to cause pervasive distress in almost anyone'.

In summary

As we have seen in this chapter there is a lot of overlap between PTS and PTSD. I hope you'll find it reassuring to know that PTS is considered a natural and normal reaction to 'abnormal' events and that PTSD, while enormously distressing and debilitating at the time, can be the very thing that can act as the catalyst for post-traumatic growth (PTG), as we'll see in the next chapter.

CHAPTER 2
What is meant by
post-traumatic growth?

Post-traumatic growth (PTG) is the positive change that can happen in the wake of a traumatic event. When people go through trauma, alongside the distress they feel, they often discover something they value about themselves and change in ways that can add up to a personal transformation. PTG is the positive psychological change that comes about as a result of the struggle with highly challenging life circumstances. When we go through major adversity it is normal to fear that it will break us but in time people generally return to their previous level of well-being. PTG goes beyond recovery to something more positive emerging from the negative experience. Not simply a return

FOCUSON **EXAMPLES OF PTG**

'I question everything now. Is this the type of work I'm supposed to be doing? There's so many things to question.'

'I see it as a second chance for life. My husband and I are adopting.'

These are the words of survivors of the plane that crash-landed on the Hudson River in New York in 2009. They are also examples of post-traumatic growth.

to baseline after a period of suffering, it is an experience of improved functioning. Research suggests that a traumatic event doesn't have to doom us to eternal suffering, instead it can act as a springboard to a life of higher well-being and deeper meaning. People who've experienced PTG talk about feeling stronger and having gained unexpected benefits from the adversity. This personal growth, many examples of which feature in this book, often marks a genuine turning point in their lives.

In what ways does PTG change your life?

Post-traumatic growth is both a process of transformation and a potential outcome after a period of grave adversity. There are three major areas of life in which people experience change:

1. Change in the self. Rising to the challenge of getting through the crisis reveals abilities in ourselves; this alters our self-perception. People grow in strength and wisdom and become more accepting of their vulnerabilities. This stronger self helps to protect them from future stresses.

2. Change in relationships. People experience a greater need for connection, feel closer to their loved ones, value their friends and family more, and have more compassion toward others.

CASESTUDY PTG AFTER CANCER

A publisher was diagnosed with cancer after finding a lump in her breast. Then her partner also received a cancer diagnosis. 'When the consultant told me: "You have breast cancer, we think it is stage 2," I was running a small business and we agreed that I would continue to work for as long as I felt able to. Along with the fear of dying of cancer, the interesting thing was that I also felt immense relief. "I can let go now." I had been feeling burdened by the business for some time but didn't want to let people down. The cancer became my friend in that curious way – it gave me a good reason to stop. Now Andrew and I have both finished our treatments and are well.

'Cancer brought about a profound change. It pushed me off my feeling that in order to be loved, to be a good person,

3. Change in philosophy of life. The impact of adversity leads to shifts in priorities and worldview. People re-evaluate what is important to them and have a greater appreciation of life.

I hope the publisher's story above will convince you that there can be a silver lining even in life's most difficult experiences – and that with adversity can also come a sense

I needed to be perfect and shiny and well. Instead I found that my body and brain were fallible and the world didn't fall apart. People still loved me. I let go of the business and it was OK. And I feel much more in touch with life – knowledge of my own vulnerability has helped me to open to others.

'There were many positives, to the extent that if you offered me the opportunity to change my history and not have cancer, I would not take you up on it. It made me see what was important. It made me cherish my wonderful network of friends and family and community. It made both Andrew and I realize that we needed to get on with our lives and do what we wanted, now, rather than in the future. It has brought us closer. We are walking 690 miles of the pilgrimage route to Santiago de Compostela in Spain and then we plan further travels. As he said to me the other day, "You know, life feels like an adventure again."'

of expansion and transformation. PTG doesn't in any way imply an absence of distress, or being in denial of the impact of trauma. It's simply that we know now there are ways to work through these tough times to achieve growth.

The relationship between trauma and growth is not straightforward. As you may expect, sometimes the severity of the trauma, such as in the case of a genocide, can be so huge that people may never fully recover. And at the other end of the scale, in more minor, short-lived incidents, there may not be quite enough adversity to lead to the 'struggle' which induces growth. According to one of the leading experts in the field, Prof. Stephen Joseph from the University of Nottingham, the most growth is likely to occur in those who are psychologically shaken by the trauma and experiencing some degree of PTS. This might even help us view PTS in a fresh light as the engine that drives the development of PTG.

The good news is that PTG is not only common but, in fact, outnumbers reports of PTSD. It's important to mention that PTG is not universal and there is no guarantee of it. However, recognizing that suffering and growth, or personal distress and personal development, can and do co-occur raises, in itself, the likelihood of it.

If you've been through something deeply traumatic, it's probably best to have no *expectation* of PTG but simply to be receptive to the possibility of it. I've come across many cases of PTG through my work, sometimes occurring decades after the original trauma. This was the case for firefighter Tara Lal, who suffered a double tragedy in childhood with her mother's death followed by her brother's suicide (see pages 54–55).

Where did the concept of PTG come from?

The phenomenon of positive change as a result of adversity has been documented throughout history by philosophers and theologians. All the major religious traditions have something to say about how we respond to suffering but it wasn't until the 1990s that psychologists established a field of research exploring the concept of growth through adversity. The term 'post-traumatic growth' was coined by psychologists Richard Tedeschi and Lawrence Calhoun at the University of North Carolina in the mid-1990s. It is also sometimes known in psychology circles as 'adversarial growth', 'psychological growth', 'benefit finding', 'stress-related growth' and 'perceived benefits'.

The events of 9/11 significantly heightened interest in PTG. The terrorist attacks of 2001 shocked the USA to the core and left a mark on the American psyche. Yet, even in the first few months of national trauma, there were reports of positive changes. A rise in altruistic behaviour, for instance, with people coming forward to donate blood, time or money to help the survivors and bereaved.

What kind of traumatic experiences lead to PTG?

British psychologists Alex Linley and Stephen Joseph carried out one of the first reviews of PTG studies in 2004, with PTG being reported across a wide range of adversities, including:

- **Transport accidents** such as shipping disasters, car crashes, aviation incidents. See the case study of PTG after an accident on pages 124–125.
- **Natural disasters** such as hurricanes, earthquakes.
- **Interpersonal assaults** e.g. combat, sexual violence, child abuse.
- **Illnesses** such as cancer (see case study of the cancer survivor on pages 48–49), heart attacks, leukaemia, rheumatoid arthritis, multiple sclerosis, HIV/AIDS.
- **Life events** e.g. relationship breakdown, parental divorce, bereavement, emigration. See the case study on financial loss on the opposite page.

What are the main benefits of PTG?

As already mentioned, PTG leads to major change in our sense of self, relationships and life philosophy/priorities, but what about the ways in which it can benefit our lives? Richard Tedeschi and Lawrence Calhoun have mapped, in their 'transformational model' of PTG, five key areas in which growth occurs:

- **Personal strength**
- **Closer relationships**
- **Greater appreciation for life**
- **New possibilities**
- **Spiritual development**

CASESTUDY FINDING STRENGTH
AFTER FINANCIAL LOSS

A trainee osteopath from Iceland and her family lost their homes to the country's bankruptcy in 2008.

'The sudden reality was that we had virtually nothing left. My new home was taken by the bank for almost nothing. I remember once I hardly had money for food but I didn't tell anyone because most of the people closest to me had left Iceland. It was very hard to see my family give up and move abroad to start again.

'I have been through a lot in my life but the experience of losing everything financially and seeing my family go through the same has only made me stronger and more focused on what matters. Now I look back and think how the experience simplified my life. What I have realized is that what matters is love and that never goes away and sometimes is only discovered by peeling all the material stuff away. I look at my son and simply appreciate that we have food to eat and smiles on our faces. I feel stronger and view the experience as a test of my strength. Counting crabs with my son on the beach is more important than counting pennies.'

CASESTUDY A FIREFIGHTER'S STORY

'As a young girl, I felt lost, isolated and confused by grief as a result of the death of my mother, so I clung to my elder brother. He became my rock when everything else in my life had given way beneath me. When I was 17 he took his own life. My fragile world shattered around me and I found myself engulfed in a tidal wave of grief.

'For many years I tried to put it to one side. It was only in my thirties that the pain of my childhood started to play itself out in my life when, as a firefighter, I attended a call to a suicide followed by a colleague attempting suicide. With the help of a psychologist I actively turned toward all the fear. Digging into my past and reliving the grief as an adult made me question life and, in amongst the darkness of grief, I found beauty and wonder in the simplest of things and in doing so found myself, my passions and my strength.

'Ever so slowly a transformation occurred within me. I realized that the scars I held had given me the gift of compassion and with that came a unique insight and ability to connect. I knew then that connection formed the essence of life. For years I couldn't think of or talk about suicide so I undertook training in suicide-prevention skills and found myself talking someone out of taking their own life. We spoke several times over months. Almost a year later she rang to thank me. She said: 'I don't know how you knew, but you knew.' In that moment all my past experiences made sense. I not only could, but more importantly *had* a burning desire to make a difference in the world and maybe I could combine all my skills and past experience to do that. I started working with the Black Dog Institute to help build resilience in firefighters and reduce the incidence of PTSD and suicide in emergency service workers.

'Then, even though I had no writing experience, I began to write the story of my brother and me, documented in the book *Standing on My Brother's Shoulders*. Something inherent drove me for I was living my meaning and purpose in life. That was my brother's gift to me. The face I showed to the world and my internal world became fused and I found the strength to live the life I wanted to, not the life others expected of me. For years I only saw what life took from me. Now I see what it has given me.'

Tara's story reveals many of the features of PTG – a deep sense of meaning and purpose and a desire to make a difference in the world. These are examples of eudaimonic well-being, which you can read more about in Chapter 5.

As it is normal for the positive and negative to co-exist, it may well be that while you are still going through symptoms of trauma, you may recognize some of the traits listed on page 52 beginning to take root in your own life. If so, you may already be on a PTG journey. And if not I hope these feel like worthwhile qualities to keep in mind as you make your way through the most testing of times.

Increased personal strength

There is definitely truth in the old adage that 'what doesn't kill you makes you stronger'. Dealing with a traumatic experience can consume every ounce of energy you possess and still people are able to find unknown reserves of strength within them to keep going. While facing up to the challenge of adversity can leave you feeling weak, at the same time it may actually be strengthening you in all kinds of ways – maybe initially unseen. A traumatic experience can test you to your limits but having gone through one trying situation will equip you for future difficult events. It also helps you get to know yourself better and discover what you're really capable of.

Trauma survivors often talk about having gained a deeper understanding of themselves and an increased sense of authenticity. They know who they really are and how they've changed for the better. They also refer to feeling more alive, open, empathetic and humble and that they have more compassion toward others having been through trauma themselves. This can result in a greater feeling of confidence and maturity, particularly for those who go through trauma at a young age.

Closer and more meaningful relationships

Trauma is just as much a test of our relationships as it is of ourselves. The tough times can bring you closer as you open up to loved ones and receive their support. Some relationships, however, may not survive the crisis for all kinds of reasons. For example, some people simply might not feel strong enough to face up to what you have gone through; some might not be open enough to accept a change in the dynamic of your relationship with them. It can be disappointing to discover that some people you thought would be there for you turn out not to be. But, on the other hand, you may be pleasantly surprised at unexpected kindness from others, including strangers, who rally around to support you. I remember when my mother was seriously ill I got a phone call telling me to come quickly to the hospital as the medics were concerned about her condition. It was the worst drive of my life. Three hours later I sprinted onto the ward only to find her bed was empty. A nurse, spotting my distress, scooped me up from the floor and put her arm through mine to walk me around to the other side of the ward where my mother had been moved. I'll never forget

CASESTUDY BIRTH OF A DISABLED CHILD LEADS TO MAJOR SHIFTS IN RELATIONSHIPS

When a marketing executive discovered she was expecting a child with Down's Syndrome, she was encouraged to terminate the pregnancy. She decided instead to go ahead.

'My priorities changed overnight and although it was a very stressful time, my partner and I became closer than ever. If I'd felt protective over my immediate family before, I suddenly felt a thousand times more so. My little family unit was what was important in life.

'During the last months of pregnancy, my life changed considerably. I lost a lot of "friends" – some never even contacted me after they heard the news about the baby – and I was left with only a handful of good friends. My life was stripped back but somehow it felt good – through this ordeal, through this unknown, terrifying entity, I discovered my true friends, my true self and I suddenly felt really strong.

'My family is what is important to me and I am now conscious of true friendship and feel very grateful for it.'

her kindness. Going through a traumatic experience opens you up to the importance of other people for our well-being. The superficialities of life, whether stressing to meet deadlines or preserve appearances, are swept away and you may discover a new sense of community, such as with fellow trauma survivors in support groups and internet forums. This was the experience of a local government worker in Wales after major surgery to remove a brain tumour. 'Trauma certainly helps you to sort out who your real soulmates are. And it allows you to meet amazing new people in hospital and fellow survivors as you watch each other go through rehabilitation in slow, often circular patterns. You all get used to living in "setback city" – one step forward, two back – as you learn to walk and talk and think again.'

A new appreciation for life

It's no surprise when an adversity rocks your world, such as a diagnosis of serious illness or a financial crisis, that it can prompt you to question everything, change your philosophy of life and search for new meaning. It can also greatly increase your appreciation of life itself, especially if you have been faced with the reality of your own mortality during your trauma. For some people this can act as a wake-up call, reminding them just how precious our time here on earth is and prompting them to reflect deeply on how best to make use of the time that they have remaining.

New priorities and possibilities

There is often a sense of life 'before' and 'after' a traumatic event. No surprise then that, as your life changes, so too do your priorities. You may well become less concerned with trivia which might impact on how you want to spend your time, the work you want to do and even the people you want to be around. The local government worker mentioned on

CASESTUDY LIVING WITH A LIFE-LIMITING CONDITION

An HR professional had the shock of his life when he went to the doctor to get the results of a kidney test. 'When I was told that I would only have kidney function for another 10 years, it seemed the world had collapsed on top of me. It was like an early death sentence. It was the beginning of a long battle and a fight for the life I wanted to continue to live with passion and joy. My illness has helped me understand life in all its immense beauty and fragility. Today I practise a form of gratitude every day that allows me to appreciate more and more the unexpected, wonderful surprises that life brings us as well as the immense kindness and tenderness of small gestures from others.'

page 59 lost her career but gained a new attitude. 'Before my trauma I was incredibly career-orientated, climbing ever higher. I'd think: 'Let us just get through this hour, this day, this month, this year and everything will be easier.' Now I have the opposite attitude to time; it's not something to be got through but something to be enjoyed. An hour to walk around the lake, a day for creating teaching resources, a week to explore a coastal cycle path. I don't need to hang on in there for futuristic pleasures and relaxation. I enjoy what I'm doing.'

Trauma reconnects you with what's truly important in life. You may want to spend more time on meaningful pursuits, whether that's spending time with your family, helping people in need, or ensuring you get more down time just to 'be'. This opens up a deeper kind of happiness known in psychology as 'eudaimonic well-being', which comes from living a life of meaning and purpose and which we explore in more depth on pages 132–135.

Spiritual development

A life-changing trauma, such as facing the reality of our mortality, can also result in major changes in spirituality and our philosophy in life. The crisis can prompt us to ask the big existential questions: What is the meaning of life? Is there a God? What happens when we die? What is the purpose of my life?

FOCUS ON LEARNING FROM THE DYING

The Top 5 Regrets of the Dying is a book by Bronnie Ware, an Australian palliative care nurse. Her job involved looking after patients in the last weeks of their lives. She had many special conversations during these times. 'I learnt never to underestimate someone's capacity for growth when they are faced with their own mortality. Each experienced a variety of emotions but every patient found their peace before they departed.' When she asked about regrets or things they would do differently, common themes surfaced again and again.

1. I wish I hadn't worked so hard.
2. I wish I'd stayed in touch with my friends.
3. I wish I'd let myself be happier.
4. I wish I'd had the courage to express my true self.
5. I wish I'd lived a life true to my dreams instead of what others expected of me.

These regrets reflect much of the growth experienced by the people who have shared their stories in this chapter. PTG helps people live an authentic life in touch with what is truly important to them.

Survivors often talk about experiencing spiritual growth, developing a faith in something bigger than themselves as they go through their 'long dark night of the soul'. They may decide to pray or meditate, or find comfort in the religion of their childhood or a new faith. The tsunami survivor felt a strong spiritual sensation when she came close to drowning. 'Instead of feeling any sense of panic, I felt that everything was simply fine as it was and that I would live on through my love for others and theirs for me. This has left me with a strong sense that, whatever religion we may practise, love is really all that matters and, as such, is the ultimate power.'

Some people also feel gratitude toward a divine entity for helping them get through the crisis. A sepsis survivor, who suffered the loss of both legs and several fingers, was sustained by his faith in God during seven gruelling months in hospital. 'We have been tested greatly by this episode in our life but my wife and I have found that hope and trust and our belief in God helped us through the various stages of recovery and into new seasons in our life.'

You may not necessarily experience all five of the areas of growth identified in this chapter but psychologists Tedeschi and Calhoun estimate that up to 90 per cent of trauma survivors will experience change in one of these dimensions. As mentioned by the brain tumour survivor on page 59, the journey from trauma to growth is often a case of one step forward and two back. It is highly unlikely to be the instant makeover so beloved of TV and lifestyle magazines. Trauma sends out ripples that can continue to have an impact for years. Equally, the growth may be a long time in coming but no less substantial when it finally arrives.

How does PTG happen?

PTG is thought to involve a dismantling and rebuilding of our internal world. Much of the early thinking around PTG is based on the 'Shattered Assumptions' theory (1992) developed by Prof. Ronnie Janoff-Bulman at the University of Massachusetts Amherst. The theory states that trauma destroys our benevolent view that the world is a safe, predictable and just place and that we are good and worthy people. According to the theory, trauma can cause us to reject the view that, if we do the right thing, all will turn out well in the end. Traumatic experiences, such as the death of a child or being critically injured, break these assumptions. PTG develops by engaging with this new and painful reality. Rebuilding our internal world inevitably involves a form of cognitive restructuring which includes major shifts in the way we view life and ourselves.

The process starts by trying to make sense of the trauma, which can prompt a re-evaluation of our core beliefs. In the early stages, unwelcome, automatic thoughts triggered by the traumatic experience feel intrusive. But later on this rumination shifts into something more constructive as people find some meaning in the adversity and gravitate toward a place of acceptance about their changed world, gaining wisdom and well-being along the way.

Making meaning out of the suffering is a key part of the PTG process. Highly influential in our understanding of meaning is Viktor Frankl, an Austrian psychiatrist who was imprisoned in Nazi concentration camps during World War Two and lost his wife and most of his immediate family. In his book *Man's Search for Meaning* Frankl states that 'Everything can be taken from a man but . . . the last of the human freedoms – to choose one's attitude in any given set of circumstances.' We may not always be able to control what happens to us but we can control the meaning we give to it and find some value in it. Changing how we think about what happens is at the core of modern resilience training. Finding a way to regard the adversity as a challenge to rise to will help with the process of growth.

Self-actualization – 'The actualizing tendency'

Another approach to PTG comes from British psychologists Stephen Joseph and Alex Linley, who worked at the University of Warwick in the mid-2000s. According to their 'organismic valuing theory', people have a propensity to growth and are motivated to fulfil their potential. Adversity leads to a breakdown in the beliefs that form our identity, and PTS is the signal that we need to process the new trauma-related information on a cognitive level. PTS then becomes the catalyst for PTG, as people are naturally motivated to process the traumatic experience in ways that will maximize their psychological well-being. How you rebuild your internal world and incorporate the traumatic events into your perspective on life, will determine whether or not you experience PTG.

Assimilation v Accommodation

In his book *What Doesn't Kill Us* (2011) Stephen Joseph uses the example of a shattered vase (see box opposite) to illustrate how the process of PTG operates:

- **assimilation**, which will take you back to where you were pre-trauma, albeit in a more fragile state (like a vase re-formed from many broken fragments)
- **accommodation**, which has the potential to spur you on to positive growth and higher functioning (like a new artwork made from the fragments of the vase)

Assimilation occurs when a person maintains their pre-trauma worldview and does not alter their mental frameworks. An example of this might be a homemaker,

FOCUS ON UNDERSTANDING THE 'SHATTERED VASE' METAPHOR

As mentioned opposite, Prof. Stephen Joseph uses a brilliant metaphor of mending or recycling a broken vase to explain the processes of assimilation and accommodation in response to trauma.

Imagine a lovely piece of porcelain falling and breaking into pieces. If you pick up the pieces and very carefully stick them back together, the vase may end up looking more or less like it did before, but the truth is that it will be weaker, held together with glue or sticking tape, and will be more likely to break again or to leak. This is **assimilation**. You and your life may look the same but in reality you are much more fragile.

If, on the other hand, you choose to collect all the pieces and make something new out of them such as a beautiful mosaic, the end result will be something unique and valuable in its own right. Something new has emerged from the old. This is **accommodation**. You will look and feel different but will be stronger as a result of accepting and working with the new reality.

who, after the death of her husband, feels she needs to carry on with the same role as before, or a business person who expects to be able to keep working full kilter after suffering a serious illness. This may be because they feel unable to come to terms fully with the tragedy but, unfortunately, it is likely to leave them all the more vulnerable to future stressful events as they have not been able to renegotiate their assumptions about life.

Accommodation, on the other hand, happens when someone is able to face up to and engage actively with the new reality of their post-trauma situation and rebuild their mental framework to accommodate the trauma within it. An example of this would be a widow accepting that she needs to take a new role in providing for the family after the loss of her husband, or the business person realizing that they have to alter their working patterns and/or workload after illness.

Is PTG a purely psychological process?

The gains that come with PTG extend beyond the mind to benefit the body too. Often we take our bodies for granted but the shock of a trauma such as a cancer diagnosis can reconnect us with the physical and prompt us to take better care of our bodies. Engaging with exercise, nutrition and rest not only supports healing but can help the body become stronger, more resilient and function better than it did before, as we'll see in the next chapter. Studies have shown better immune system functioning and lower cortisol levels as some of the positive physical outcomes of PTG.

We've now reached the turning point in the book where our focus shifts from learning about adversity to facilitating PTG itself. Although you may have had little or no control over the circumstances that resulted in your trauma, you do have choices over the future. What counts now is not so much what happened to you but what happens next. The chapters that follow draw on positive psychology, the science of resilience and well-being, to take you on a journey that will show you how to rise to the challenge of trauma by:

- Coping positively while in the eye of the storm
- Strengthening your resilience for times of extreme stress
- Laying down the foundations for growth

The journey from trauma to growth is not, in real life, a simple linear one. One day you might be in 'grow' mode and the next you might be back to 'cope'. I hope that the model of cope/strengthen/grow presented here proves a useful way to help you navigate through times when you're feeling lost or overwhelmed. You may well prefer to dip into the chapters at random to find tips and tools to suit how you're feeling at the time. Choose whichever way works best for you.

CHAPTER 3
How do you cope
positively during and
after trauma?

Trauma is a complex experience which means, in truth, that there is no one-size-fits-all approach to dealing with it. So, for this and the chapters that follow, I have handpicked a selection of therapies and self-help techniques which are known for being helpful in coping with trauma, managing PTS symptoms, building resilience and ultimately increasing the likelihood of PTG.

First and foremost, whether you are in the midst of trauma or in its immediate aftermath, it's important to give yourself the time and space to have what is a natural, human response to a difficult experience. Shock, grief, sadness and a sense of shattered beliefs are completely normal and in no way indicative of any weakness or failure on your part. They are, however, signals of a need for some self-care. This is more than just routine healthcare. Self-care includes any intentional actions you take to support your physical, mental and emotional health. It's about actively making deposits into your bank of resilience by nurturing your mind, body and spirit and reaching out to loved ones and people who can help you recover. All this makes coping much easier.

What might 'coping' with trauma look like?

Every trauma has its own unique features, depending on the severity of the event, its duration and the subjective experience of the survivor, but what they have in common is that they are extremely stressful experiences that stretch and overwhelm your ability to cope.

'Positive coping' involves the strategies and actions you can take to manage and reduce the stress of these challenging situations. So how do you cope positively when you are being tested to your very limits? Let me say first that there isn't a 'right' way to cope, but there are two major coping responses, which Lazarus and Folkman describe in their transactional model of stress and coping (1984). These are:

- Emotion-focused coping
- Problem-focused coping

As you read the explanations below, try to identify your own default coping style and notice whether one of the other approaches might have something to offer you.

Emotion-focused coping

This is when your attention is on the emotional distress caused by the trauma rather than on resolving the problematic situation itself. Emotion-focused coping involves trying to reduce and manage anxiety, depression, fear and other negative emotional responses. Coping strategies such as confiding in a sympathetic friend and having a good cry help us feel better even if they don't solve the issue. Not every adversity has a solution to it, of course, nor is it within our total control – bereavement or a diagnosis of terminal illness, for example – so allowing yourself to feel and express emotions can help you adjust to the situation. Reaching out to a trusted friend or a counsellor for moral support and a shoulder to lean on are ways into emotion-focused coping. Other forms include meditation, listening to music, physical activity such as going for a walk, journalling or expressing your emotions through acts of creativity or humour. Dark humour, for example, is often used by those working in the emergency services as a way of coping with the trauma and tragedy they routinely witness. Beware, however, of the less healthy forms of emotion-focused coping such as drowning your sorrows in alcohol or over-indulging in comfort food.

Emotion-focused coping can be particularly useful in the early stages of PTS to self-soothe during high emotional distress or in circumstances that will not change and where you need to learn to accept the situation as it is.

Problem-focused coping

This coping method involves taking practical steps to move forward and resolve the issue, and can often be most helpful after an initial period of emotion-focused coping. People using problem-focused coping try to deal directly with the cause of adversity to reduce or eliminate the stress involved.

It's a more active form of coping, appropriate for situations in which you can exercise some control, such as in the case of a business failure or a toxic relationship. By shouldering the responsibility for your own well-being and developing a plan of action, you have a map to navigate your way forward. Seeking out information, evaluating the pros and cons, learning new skills and applying a solutions focus are all positive forms of taking control.

Does avoidance coping help?

PTS sufferers often engage in avoidance coping, trying to stay away from anything associated with the trauma. Although the idea of 'avoiding' your PTS may, at first, sound like a negative way to react – and it would be if you did it on a permanent basis – in the short term it can be a helpful way of disengaging from the source of distress when it's at its most overwhelming. This could take the form, for example, of going to the cinema to lose yourself in a film for a couple of hours or doing something else you like that acts as a distraction from your distress and gives you a break to regroup and marshal your inner resources. Where it becomes dysfunctional is if, over the long term, you continue to distract yourself, such as with alcohol, drugs, overwork or sex, to avoid dealing with the situation. It's a good idea to look to some of the problem-focused coping strategies to find a way to move forward.

What do you need to keep going through trauma?

The hierarchy of needs (1943) is a well-known theory in the psychology world. Abraham Maslow's quest to understand human motivation led him to formulate a list of basic needs that have to be fulfilled in order to maximize psychological health (see diagram below). The bottom layers of the pyramid represent deficiency needs, where there is a lack of something that needs to be satisfied before moving to the upper levels, which are needs for growth. I think this hierarchy feels particularly relevant to managing PTS symptoms and the journey from trauma to growth.

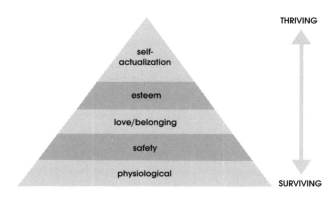

THRIVING

- self-actualization
- esteem
- love/belonging
- safety
- physiological

SURVIVING

Doing what we can simply to *survive* trauma is the clear priority early on in the recovery process. This involves tending to the physiological needs at the bottom of the pyramid, such as food and sleep. Once our basic physical needs are covered, the next layer up is the need for safety – not only physical safety but a sense of psychological, social and economic safety to regain stability after trauma. Once the lower needs are met, then we can begin to move further up toward thriving.

Tending to the body is a crucial first step to recovery. Trauma lives in our bodies as well as our minds according to Bessel van der Kolk, author of *The Body Keeps the Score*. The body–mind connection is frequently underrated in the traditional Western understanding of health. Our emotions, for example, come with physical expressions – fear with a racing heart, sadness with tears, or anger with muscle tension and a clenched jaw. Traumatized people often have trouble sensing what is going on in their bodies and yet this is important for recovery. As van der Kolk puts it, 'Trauma victims cannot recover until they become familiar with and befriend the sensations in their bodies.'

Fortunately, the body can also be used as a tool to facilitate recovery from trauma and raise well-being. The rest of this chapter offers a range of ways to help you fulfil your body's needs and enhance your physical well-being before going on to address the 'higher' needs in later chapters, all of which can put you on the path to growth through adversity.

What physical steps can you take to help you feel better?

Trauma is exhausting. You may feel *emotionally* drained so self-care following trauma is especially important to keep your body strong and healthy. Admittedly, it is easier said than done to look after your body if you are in a state of anxiety, depression or hyperarousal. One thing I did when I was in the eye of the storm was to book myself weekly massages at the local college of bodywork. Physical self-care involves:

Healthy food and drink

- Eating fresh, seasonal food with at least five portions a day of fruit and vegetables.
- Keeping your water intake up to stay well hydrated. Mental exhaustion is often a sign of dehydration.
- Lowering caffeine and sugar intake as these can make you feel more anxious than you already do.

Focusing on nutrition will not only help to maintain your physical health but also positively impact your mood and therefore mental health.

Physical awareness and activity

Good mental health is built on the foundations of physical health, and regular exercise is a powerful way to improve your mood. Psychologist Tal Ben-Shahar from Harvard

University goes as far as saying that 'not exercising is like taking depressants'. According to the Green Exercise Research Team at the University of Essex, just 5–10 minutes of physical activity in a natural environment can boost your mood. I found that strolling around my local park helped me walk my way out of depression and many of my clients have also told me how a gentle physical activity, whether that be walking, swimming or yoga, has made them feel better, despite the initial mental struggle that it can sometimes take to get started.

Often with trauma we can lose the sense of our bodies as the mind gets caught up in painful memories and emotions, making us feel detached from the world. Re-tuning into the body through physical activity can help bring you back into the present and feel more grounded. Another method is simply to notice your feet making contact with the ground as you stand and walk. Mindfulness practices, such as the 'body scan' (see pages 80–81), help raise awareness of what's going on in the whole body, not just your head.

Rest and sleep

Healing from trauma is physically and mentally draining and therefore allowing yourself to rest will recharge your batteries, help you feel better and support the recovery process. If your body is in a state of continual hyperarousal it's important to

TRYIT THE BODY SCAN

The simple meditation practice below is a way of getting back in touch with your physical self. It involves 'scanning' through each part of your body to notice what's going on without seeking to change it. As well as helping you to inhabit the whole body rather than being stuck in your head, it's a good way to 'ground' yourself. There are plenty of online audio guides to the body scan, which can take around 45 minutes. Here's a three-minute version.

- Find a quiet place to sit or lie comfortably. Close your eyes and begin by bringing your attention to your body.

- Notice the weight of your body on the chair or floor.

- Take a few deep breaths. As you breathe in, let in more oxygen, to vitalize the body. Then, as you breathe out, have a sense of relaxing more deeply.

- Notice either your feet or your buttocks on the floor. Note the sensations of them touching the floor.

- Notice your legs against the chair or floor – pressure, pulsing, heaviness, lightness.

- Notice the feeling of your back against the chair or floor.

- Bring your attention into your stomach area. If your stomach is tense or tight, let it soften. Take a breath.

- Notice your hands. Are they tense or tight? See if you can allow them to soften.

- Notice your arms. Feel any sensation that is present. Let your shoulders relax.

- Notice your neck and throat. Let them be soft. Relax.

- Soften your jaw. Let your face and facial muscles relax.

- Then take notice of your whole body. Take one more breath.

- Be aware of your whole body as best you can. Take a breath. And then, when you're ready, open your eyes.

Adapted from: The Greater Good Science Center, University of California, Berkeley.

find ways to counter-balance this, as this will allow you to sleep better too. Sleep is the ultimate restorer so if yours is disturbed it's a good idea to establish a relaxing bedtime routine and try sleep hygiene practices such as:

- Switching off electronic devices at least an hour before bedtime and keep smartphones etc. out of your bedroom.
- Avoiding caffeine, alcohol and nicotine close to bedtime.
- Doing enough physical exercise during the early part of the day so that you feel naturally sleepy later on.

How can you make friends with the parasympathetic nervous system?

As explained on page 21, the sympathetic nervous system (SNS) is constantly being fired by trauma, putting us into the state of 'fight' or 'flight'. One practical way of managing the stress response is to activate the parasympathetic nervous system (PNS), which acts as the body's brake, restoring a state of relaxation and bringing the body back to normal resting levels of functioning. Making friends with the PNS will help attend to a sense of safety, the next layer up in Maslow's hierarchy of needs (see page 76).

A simple way of activating the PNS is via something we do automatically – breathing. Deep breathing is calming, the opposite to the shallow breathing that happens with acute stress. Deliberately taking time out to enjoy a few long, deep breaths – right down into the belly – can shift your state of mind, regulate emotions and reduce anxiety. Remember it is the exhalation that triggers the PNS so allow yourself to breathe out as fully as you breathe in.

Dr Emma Seppala from Stanford University has tested yoga-breathing meditations on military veterans suffering from PTSD. In a study published in the *Journal of Traumatic Stress* (2014) she found that this form of controlled breathing significantly reduced PTSD symptoms as well as anxiety. The veterans' startle responses calmed down indicating that they were suffering from fewer signs of hyperarousal. The study suggests that something as simple as a breathing technique can be a good – and less invasive – alternative or additional form of treatment for PTS.

How else can paying attention to our physical body help us cope after trauma?

Trauma is a 'psychophysical' experience according to Babette Rothschild, trauma specialist and author of *The Body Remembers*. The brain and body process, remember and perpetuate traumatic experiences even when there is no physical component involved in the adversity itself. Flashbacks, as was explained on page 37, involve the body reliving the trauma as though it were happening right now.

Although PTS has been traditionally regarded as a disorder of the mind, trauma experts such as Bessel van der Kolk and Peter Levine agree that the body is key in the understanding and healing of traumatic experiences. A new generation of trauma therapies has emerged that take this mind–body approach to healing. These include treatments such as:

- EMDR (Eye-Movement Desensitization and Reprocessing)
- EFT (Emotional Freedom Techniques) and other tapping therapies such as TFT (Thought Field Therapy)

TRYIT **YOGA BREATHING TECHNIQUE**

Dr Andrew Weil, a leading figure in integrative medicine, is an advocate of this simple 4–7–8 breathing practice. It's immediately relaxing, acting as an antidote to stress, and is a natural tranquillizer with benefits that accrue with practice. Sit with your back straight and place the tip of your tongue against the ridge of tissue just behind your top front teeth. Hold it there throughout the exercise. Inhale quietly through the nose and exhale audibly through the mouth.

1 First of all, exhale completely through the mouth, slightly pursing the lips to make a whoosh sound.

These therapies can bring relief in a short course of sessions without any need to dwell on the adversity itself, as is often the case with talking therapies. The memories are still there but you're no longer stuck in the moment reliving the trauma.

What is EMDR and how can it help?

EMDR was discovered quite by chance in 1987 by Dr Francine Shapiro, a psychologist from the Mental Research Institute in Palo Alto, California. She was out walking in the park while preoccupied with some painful memories

2 Close your mouth and breathe in for a count of four.

3 Hold your breath for a count of seven.

4 Exhale, making the whoosh sound, for a count of eight.

5 This is one cycle; now repeat for a further three rounds.

6 Do this practice twice a day.

Pace yourself to suit your lung capacity but always maintain the 4–7–8 ratio. With practice you can slow down and breathe more deeply. This practice also helps with sleep.

FOCUS ON WHAT HAPPENS IN AN EMDR SESSION

The treatment known as Eye-Movement Desensitization and Reprocessing (EMDR) is delivered in a course of sessions. The therapist guides the client through relaxation exercises to use in case of distress and creates an 'anchor' – a safe place to return to. The client is then asked to recall the disturbing memory and follow the therapist's finger as it passes back and forth in front of their eyes. Other forms of left–right stimulation may also be used such as taps or sounds. After each 'round' the therapist checks in with the client before continuing with the eye movements until the distress has cleared or is substantially reduced. The goal is to help the body unlock the 'frozen' traumatic memories and reprocess them. Accessing them in this way serves to 'neutralize' the memories so that the original issue is no longer disturbing and the client is able to experience more positive emotions and thoughts.

when she noticed that her eyes were moving rapidly back and forth and that this brought relief to her distress. She experimented further and found that certain eye movements reduced the intensity and anxiety of disturbing thoughts. Since then a protocol has been developed for EMDR, and it is now recommended as an effective treatment for PTSD by the World Health Organization, the American Psychiatric Association and the National Health Service in the UK.

EMDR is based on a natural function of the body – Rapid Eye Movement (REM). The mind uses REM during sleep to process the emotional experiences of the day. Traumatic memories and associated stimuli may be poorly processed and get stored in an isolated memory network as a 'memory-filing error'. REM sleep therefore fails to bring the usual relief from distress. EMDR is thought to produce an advanced stage of REM processing that can unlock the trauma. Through the eye movement the brain is able to process the emotionally charged memory and alleviate symptoms associated with it.

What is EFT and how can it help?

Since the 1980s we've witnessed the emergence of mind–body therapies collectively known as 'energy psychology', based on the concept of life force or chi/qi in traditional Chinese medicine. Among these are 'tapping therapies', which are forms of acupressure based on the same energy points as those used in acupuncture. The best known of these are Emotional Freedom Techniques (EFT), which involve gently tapping with fingertips on a sequence of meridian points on the face, hands and upper body while tuning in to a particular event or memory that holds distress or pain.

TRYIT EFT: THE BASIC RECIPE

The 'basic recipe' is an elementary EFT technique that can be used to help with all kinds of emotional issues. Gary Craig's website www.emofree.com has full instructions and a video to guide you.

- Bring to mind the source of distress and rate its intensity on a scale of 1–10.

- Design a phrase that describes the experience using this format: 'Even though I have (e.g. a fear of drowning), I deeply and completely accept myself.'

- Say the phrase three times while tapping using two or three fingers on the fleshy point on the side of the hand (the 'karate chop' point).

- Choose a short version of this sentence as the 'reminder phrase' (e.g. 'fear of drowning').

- Next tap each of the following acupressure points 5–7 times while saying the reminder phrase out loud:

- Top of the head

- Beginning of the eyebrow (inner edge)

- Side of the eye

- Under the eye

- Under the nose

- Chin point

- Beginning of the collarbone (inner edge)

- Under the arm (on a line with the nipple)

- Test the intensity of the issue by rating it again from 1–10 to get a sense of progress. Continue with more rounds until the intensity goes down to zero or plateaus at a low level.

The evidence for EFT's efficacy as a treatment for PTS looks promising. There have been several randomized control trials conducted with military veterans which show substantial improvements in their symptoms of PTSD, anxiety and depression, and a reduction in their levels of cortisol, the stress hormone.

Sometimes referred to as 'psychological acupressure', EFT reduces the intensity of emotional trauma, lowering stress levels and the symptoms of hyperarousal. An American named Gary Craig devised EFT in the 1990s, inspired by Thought Field Therapy (TFT), a tapping technique developed by psychologist Dr Roger Callahan. EFT is based on the notion that the cause of negative emotions is a disruption in the body's energy system and that tapping on meridians will help to release blockages and clear unresolved issues. The advantages of using tapping are that it is simple, non-invasive and rapid-acting. EFT is effective within a few sessions without the need to revisit the traumatic experience over and over again, flooding the body with stress hormones each time. In a similar way to EMDR, you will still remember the trauma but it is no longer as charged as it was before. EFT can be self-administered but it is advisable to work with a qualified therapist first of all so that you can experience EFT within a safe space before using it as a self-help tool.

In summary

The major theme in this chapter has been that the body can be used as an *instrument* for healing trauma. The positive news is that the benefits don't stop there. Dr Kate Hefferon from the University of East London has identified, through her work with cancer survivors, three main ways in which people can also experience PTG *related* to the body – there can be some kind of physical improvement post-trauma. Known as 'corporeal post-traumatic growth', this can show up as:

- **A new, improved relationship with the body.** Having a serious illness can act as a 'wake-up call' to stop taking our bodies for granted and treat them with kindness. As we become more aware of the body, we are more likely to handle it with increased care. Taking exercise, for example, can result in regaining and even surpassing previous levels of physical functioning.
- **Greater awareness of health-related behaviour.** Trauma survivors have a stronger sense of the importance of the body and are therefore more likely to engage in healthy practices such as eating well and give up damaging habits like smoking and excessive alcohol consumption.
- **Stronger in mind as well as body.** After experiencing trauma many people report that making positive changes to their *physical health* also led to them functioning better *psychologically*, such as feeling more mentally alert and having greater optimism toward the future.

Now that we've explored a range of ways to help us cope in the eye of the storm, in the next chapter we'll look at how we can work on strengthening our resilience so that we feel better equipped to face up to what life throws at us.

CHAPTER 4

How can you strengthen
your resilience to keep
going through adversity?

Bad things happen. But while some people go under when faced with adversity, others find a way through and are able to bounce back from the crisis. The key difference between these groups is what is known as *resilience* – having the inner strength to keep going while the winds of adversity threaten to topple you. In this chapter we turn our attention from body-based practices to some of the more mind-focused therapies that can fortify us to move through adversity and sow the seeds of growth.

What exactly do we mean by resilience?

Resilience is about maintaining and regaining psychological well-being in the face of adversity, trauma, tragedy and other major sources of stress such as serious health problems or overwhelming work pressures. There is a wide variety of definitions of resilience but psychologists agree on there being three main types:

- **Resistance resilience.** The ability to stand strong while going through adversity, like having your feet planted firmly on the ground.

- **Recovery resilience**, also known as 'bouncebackability'. Being able to rebound to the level of functioning you had prior to the adversity, like the tree that bends and sways in a storm.

- **Reconfiguration resilience.** The changes that occur through adversity which can improve someone's capacity to cope with subsequent challenges. This can be a stepping stone to PTG.

The good news is that resilience is not something you're either born with or not – it's something you can learn. Dr Karen Reivich, co-author of *The Resilience Factor*, describes resilience as 'a group of positive characteristics, abilities and resources' and teaches seven skills – emotion regulation, impulse control, optimism, flexible thinking, self-efficacy (confidence in problem-solving), empathy and reaching out (to take appropriate risks). Neither is resilience some rare quality. Prof. Ann Masten, from the University of Minnesota, refers to it as 'ordinary magic' because resilience arises from a range of common factors such as close relationships or a brain that's functioning OK.

Resilience is much more common than you might imagine. Prof. George Bonanno from Columbia University has carried out research into traumatic experiences such as the death of a spouse and the events of 9/11. His research suggests that the most widespread reaction to trauma or loss is not PTSD as you might first think, but is, in fact, resilience. Even with troops heading into a war zone, the most 'common' consequence of high adversity is a brief episode of depression and anxiety before a return to previous levels of functioning. This particular insight comes from Prof. Martin Seligman, who works with the United States Army on the Comprehensive Soldier Family Fitness (CSFF) programme, which aims to build resilience in service personnel and their families.

The relationship, however, between resilience and PTG is not clear-cut. Some studies suggest that the higher your resilience, the less likely you are to experience PTG as you have less of the struggle with trauma, the mechanism that triggers PTG. I prefer to take the pragmatic view that the actions that build resilience will also strengthen your chances of the positive transformation that is PTG.

Can we take steps to build resilience?

The first thing to note is that you already have a resilience resource available to you and that is YOU. The way you coped in the past will help you cope in the future. As a starter try this: Take a few minutes to think back over your life decade by decade. Then get a pen and a large piece of paper, and draw a lifeline, plotting the major events and turning points on it. Now ask yourself what you did that helped you get through the difficult times. What can you learn from the past that might serve you in the future? The SSRI exercise on pages 98–99 draws on the precious resource that is your previous experience.

Who is your Resilience Hero?

Think about someone in your life who could serve as a role model of resilience for you. Maybe a member of your family – an aunt, uncle or grandparent? Someone you know through work? Or even someone in public life? What strengths did they draw upon to help them through their time of crisis?

For me it would be my grandmother, an agricultural worker in northern France with 12 children and a farm to look after. During World War Two, while being evacuated from the farm, she survived a piece of shrapnel lodging in her neck after an air raid. She was a Resilience Hero for me because of her stoical, down-to-earth nature and her great spirit – she was able to find lightness even in the gloomiest times.

Another personal Resilience Hero for me would be Nelson Mandela, who was incarcerated for 27 years but somehow kept the faith and went on to become President of South Africa on his release. His strengths must surely include perseverance, justice and leadership, demonstrated in his own PTG journey from surviving prison to thriving as the nation's leader.

Whose tale of endurance inspires *you*? And what lessons can you learn from how they managed and bounced back from their time of adversity?

Can mindfulness help build resilience?

Trauma can hold us in a pattern of reliving distress over and
over. When we have persistent upsetting experiences, we
can end up reacting more emotionally to situations that
others might not find disturbing. This can feel very intense
and make it more difficult to manage our emotions and
behaviour. The key difference between a traumatized brain
and a resilient one is this 'emotional reactivity'. Mindfulness
is an ancient form of mind-training that can help address
this difficult issue.

- **Strengths** you drew upon? Your inner resources such as courage and perseverance.

- **Resources** you turned to? The external sources you relied on for guidance, inspiration or support. This could be friends, family, colleagues, mentors, professionals, support groups, helplines, internet forums and organizations.

- **Insights** you found useful? Positive ideas, perspectives and philosophies that helped you through. It could even be a phrase such as 'This too will pass,' or the PTG classic, 'What doesn't kill you makes you stronger.'

Adapted from *Find Your Power*, Chris Johnstone, 2010

Originally a spiritual practice in Buddhism, mindfulness meditation has evolved into a secular practice for health, largely through the clinical work of Dr Jon Kabat-Zinn. Mindfulness means being present and Kabat-Zinn's interpretation is based on awareness as 'paying attention in a particular way, in the present moment, on purpose, non-judgementally'. In the 1970s Kabat-Zinn began testing mindfulness techniques for the management of chronic pain and other difficult-to-treat conditions at the University of Massachusetts Medical Center. He then went on to develop an eight-week programme of mindfulness, body awareness and yoga, known as Mindfulness-Based Stress Reduction (MBSR).

Mindfulness focuses attention on awareness of the inside and its relationship to the outside – noticing the thoughts, sights, sounds, smells, tastes and touch that we experience; and accepting all such experience non-judgmentally even if it is painful. With practice, this can enhance our ability to notice what's going on without being sucked into the drama of it, so we become more of an observer of our thoughts and feelings. This type of awareness can help to strengthen resilience in two main ways:

- With **reactivity.** Mindfulness can help interrupt the vicious cycle of looping thoughts, feelings and behaviours reinforcing each other. With practice it helps you become more of an observer, creating a gap between what happens and how you react so that there is greater potential for a more balanced response. This helps to dampen down emotional reactivity.

- With **rumination**. Traumatic experiences can keep you trapped in the past, brooding over what happened, or anxiously over-thinking the future. When you are stuck in a thinking track that pulls you down, winds you up or stresses you out, mindfulness can help you gain some distance from the domination of trauma-related intrusive thoughts and feelings and instead remain calm and more in the moment.

Mindfulness approaches now form part of a variety of mental health programmes and these can be useful for trauma survivors to address PTS symptoms and associated issues such as depression and anxiety. The following courses are worth investigating:

MBSR (mindfulness-based stress reduction) has been shown to help people manage the stress that is associated with physical health conditions and is now a recognized treatment for anxiety and depression, frequently present in PTSD sufferers.

MBCT (mindfulness-based cognitive therapy) draws upon both mindfulness and cognitive therapy techniques (for these, see pages 104–105) and aims to reduce the risk of relapsing into depression.

ACT (acceptance and commitment therapy) helps people develop psychological flexibility to accept what has happened and facilitate behaviour change (see the Try It box on page 119).

TRYIT A BASIC MINDFULNESS EXERCISE

This exercise is a simple introduction to mindfulness:

- Find a comfortable position either lying down or sitting
  cross-legged with a straight back and shoulders relaxed.

- Ask yourself: 'What is going on with me at the moment?'

- Allow yourself to be with whatever arises for you.
  Acknowledge what you notice with gentleness and
  kindness. For example, 'This is a moment of sadness,' or
  'I'm noticing anger in this moment.' And in the spirit of
  self-compassion, remind yourself that this is part of life,
  'It's OK to feel like this, it's part of the human experience.'

- Sounds and bodily sensations may also call for your
  attention and, as best as you can, simply notice these
  experiences with openness and curiosity as they come
  and go, flux and change.

A note of caution – mindfulness involves leaning into
experience, and this raised awareness does carry a risk of
triggering initial distress or the emergence of unprocessed
trauma. Having said that, mindfulness can also help people

- If particular thoughts or sensations keep pushing for your attention, see if it's possible to allow that to be OK, without judging yourself or giving yourself a hard time.

- Then, when you're ready, invite your attention to notice the sensations of the body and the pattern of your breathing. Just follow the rhythmic movement and return to the breath whenever the mind wanders, which it will do.

- If strong emotions or memories of painful events occur, see if it's possible to acknowledge these as well as any related sensations in the body and say something like, 'I can notice this is fear, and feel it in my chest. My heart is beating faster' etc. Then gently allow your awareness to drop back to your breathing, placing one hand on your belly, if this feels comfortable, and watching each new breath in and old breath out. Continue to use the breath as a place to return to when the mind gets caught up with thinking or worrying, so that these memories and feelings gradually decrease in intensity and frequency.

increase their distress tolerance so that they are more able to 'stay with' memories and symptoms that come up. It's advisable to join a mindfulness course run by a qualified instructor who can guide you through any difficulties.

Which psychological therapy is most recommended for resilience and recovery?

Cognitive-behavioural therapy (CBT) is at the core of many resilience programmes and is the most widely prescribed psychological therapy for PTSD. This talking therapy is based on the interaction between thoughts, emotions and behaviours. How the way you think (cognition) affects how you feel (emotion) and how you act (behaviour) and vice versa in each case. This can escalate so, for example, someone who *feels* nervous about a meeting may *think* that they might not be able to make their points clearly and that might make them *feel* more anxious, which in turn might make them *think* that it will be a disaster, which might make them *behave* by not going at all. CBT can help you understand how certain thoughts about your trauma can trigger PTS symptoms. By challenging and replacing negative automatic thoughts that trauma survivors have, such as 'Nowhere is safe', 'I'm going mad' or 'I'm dead inside', CBT may help them learn to cope with feelings of anger, fear and guilt.

The aim of CBT is to identify the blind spots in our thinking patterns that can trigger a big emotional reaction, by falling into thinking traps such as these:

All-or-nothing thinking: Viewing things in extreme or in black and white, such as thinking 'This mistake will ruin everything.'

Catastrophizing: Predicting the worst outcome possible. 'My heart is beating so fast it must mean I'm going to die.'

Emotional reasoning: Mistaking feelings for facts and believing that what you feel must be true, so if you feel like a failure it is because you are.

Jumping to conclusions: Making a negative interpretation of a situation even though there are no definite facts to support your assumption.

Mental filtering: Picking out a single negative detail, dwelling on it and therefore viewing the whole situation as negative.

Personalizing: Seeing yourself as the cause of some negative external event when you had little or no responsibility.

How can positive psychology build resilience?

Positive psychology is a practical science that not only builds well-being but is also known as the science of resilience. Many of its evidence-based practices can feed your reservoir of resilience. Three areas are especially helpful:

- recognizing and applying your strengths
- cultivating and enjoying more positive emotions
- practising optimism

FOCUS ON UNDERSTANDING THE ABC OF RESILIENCE

An important CBT-based skill taught on many resilience courses is what is known as the ABC. This helps people understand the relationship between what happens and its impact on our thoughts, feelings and behaviour.

A: Activating event – an adversity or event that tests your resilience. These are the facts of the situation.

B: The heat-of-the-moment **Belief** about what happened.

C: The **Consequences** for emotions (how you felt) and behaviour (what you did).

We tend to think that when adversity strikes, it has direct consequences on how we feel and behave, that we

Recognizing your strengths

We all have strengths as well as weaknesses but a crisis often means that we lose sight of the positive side of our nature. Strengths like courage, perseverance and hope can come into their own when you are navigating tough times. These qualities can be deployed to build resilience. Clinical psychologist Dr Tayyab Rashid, from the University go straight from A (the 'Activating Event') to C (the 'Consequences'). However, there is a middle stage: this is B, the 'Belief' associated with the activating event. It is this, not the adversity itself, that drives the consequences. Consider a relationship break-up, involving two people. If person 1's belief is 'I'll never find love again' the consequences might be that they feel devastated (emotion) and withdraw from the world (behaviour). Whereas if person 2's belief is 'I'm free at last' the consequences might be somewhat different. They may feel relieved (emotion) and join a dating website (behaviour). The same adversity is at work but with different beliefs driving different consequences. We can't always do something about the adversity but we can change our beliefs about it. If we are willing to challenge how we think about the adversity this will lead to different consequences for our emotions and behaviour. An important part of resilience is therefore being flexible in our thinking.

of Toronto, suggests that you can marshal your strengths to undo troubles. A strength in kindness or social intelligence, for example, might help mend a strained relationship.

Doctors are sometimes guilty of labelling patients according to their symptoms, referring to someone as a 'depressive' for instance, but if you search for someone's strengths in addition to their symptoms, you understand more of the whole person. The strengths approach to resilience is in two parts: firstly getting to know these positive qualities in yourself, then using your strengths in life (see also the box opposite).

Cultivating positive emotions

Emotions are not just something we feel, they also serve a purpose. Negative emotions act as our survival mechanism in that they alert us to danger. Anger prompts us to defend ourselves ('fight') while fear makes us look for an escape ('flight'; see page 21). When you're going through a traumatic experience the very idea of having a positive emotion may seem remote, but highly resilient people are, surprisingly, able to experience positive emotions alongside negative emotions, even in difficult situations.

Prof. Barbara Fredrickson of the University of North Carolina describes the function of joy, excitement, amusement etc. as the 'inner reset button' because they counteract the cardiovascular effects of negativity such as raised blood pressure. So watching a comedy or playing a fun game with a friend can provide relief on a bad day.

Our brains are, however, wired to notice what's wrong before we notice what's right, a part of the safety mechanism that kicks in whenever we're under threat. So we're aware of the

TRY IT DISCOVER YOUR CHARACTER STRENGTHS

There are 24 universal strengths of character, according to Chris Peterson and Martin Seligman, who led a mammoth project to chart all of humanity's positive qualities. We have all of these strengths present in us and they are open for development.

Each strength is located in one of six 'virtues'. By recognizing and focusing on developing your strengths you can access these virtues. You can take the free test and find out more at www.viasurvey.org.

WISDOM	COURAGE	TRANSCENDENCE
Creativity	Bravery	Appreciation of
Curiosity	Perseverance	beauty and
Judgment	Honesty	excellence
Love of learning	Zest	Gratitude
Perspective		Hope
		Humour
		Spirituality

JUSTICE	TEMPERANCE	HUMANITY
Teamwork	Forgiveness	Love
Fairness	Humility	Kindness
Leadership	Prudence	Social
	Self-regulation	intelligence

runaway car heading our way and are not distracted by appreciating the beautiful view. As a result, when something difficult happens the combination of the nature of emotion and the 'negativity bias' means that you can easily end up mired in negative emotions such as sadness and frustration. This means that we need to apply a bit of effort to cultivate positive emotions and overcome the brain's negativity bias.

FOCUS ON PRACTICES FOR POSITIVE EMOTIONS

There is widespread scientific recognition that the following practices can increase your experience of positive emotions.

Gratitude – ask yourself these three questions daily. What is good in my life? What am I grateful for? What has gone well? Or keep a gratitude journal. Gratitude is about actively tuning in and taking notice of what is positive.

Savouring – maximize your enjoyment by slowing down and using your senses to engage fully with every positive experience. Bask, relish, marvel, luxuriate, treasure and so on.

Meditation – mindfulness and loving-kindness meditations are particularly good ways to cultivate positive emotions

Mindfulness meditation is one way to do this. Eight weeks of MBSR (see pages 100–101) has been shown to increase activity in the left prefrontal cortex, an area of the brain associated with positive emotions, and reduce the activity of the right prefrontal cortex, which is related to negative emotions. I experienced this myself through MBSR. I felt as though my brain had been subtly rewired for happiness.

and don't require mental acrobatics. See pages 102–103 for more information.

Positive relationships – cherish your loved ones and make them your priority; you need many more positive than negative emotional events in a relationship for it to flourish.

Altruism – volunteer your time to help someone out. Acts of kindness make both the giver and recipient feel good.

Time in nature – spending regular time in the great outdoors produces positive emotions in a matter of minutes.

Physical activities – exercise of any kind can provide you with an instant mood lift. Make sure it's something that brings you pleasure rather than pain.

Practising optimism

It is entirely understandable that a traumatic experience might shatter any underlying sense of optimism you have about life; it may feel hard to think positively about the future for a while. But the trouble with pessimistic thinking is that, over time, it carries a high risk of leading to depression.

Practising optimistic thinking will feed your resilience and help you orient toward PTG over the long term. And it is possible to raise your optimism level, as Martin Seligman explains in his classic book *Learned Optimism*. The neuroplasticity of the brain demonstrates that what 'fires together wires together'. This means that when brain cells communicate frequently, the connection between them strengthens. And with enough repetition these connections become automatic, whether in a positive or negative way.

The more we ruminate on a negative thought, the more entrenched that negativity becomes. This is why it can be so hard to stop depressive thoughts until we find a way of interrupting the process. We can, however, harness this pattern and learn how to think more optimistically. Although this may be a struggle at first, the more you do it the easier it will become. I think of myself as a practising optimist rather than a natural-born one and it has made a significant difference in my life.

The version of optimism that Seligman describes in *Learned Optimism* is called 'explanatory' or 'attributional style'. This is based on the way we think about the causes of events that happen to us and how we explain them to ourselves.

A **pessimist** is likely to think of the causes of a negative event as being:

- *personal* ('It's all my fault.')
- *permanent* ('It's never going to change.')
- *pervasive* ('It's ruined everything.')

An **optimist**, on the other hand, will think of the same negative event in the opposite way. The cause is

- *not personal* ('There were other factors that played a role.')
- *not permanent* ('This too will pass.')
- *not pervasive* ('Other areas of my life are going well.')

Try to challenge any patterns of pessimistic thinking that you notice in yourself and think more like an optimist using these three dimensions. After a while, it should feel more natural.

What are the three Ds of Resilience?

Earlier in this chapter we explored the ABC of resilience. Now I'd like to add another letter into this process:

The D of resilience is for

- *Disputation*
- *Distraction*
- *Distancing*

Disputation

Seligman recommends getting to know your habitual thinking patterns and challenging the negative explanations of negative events. We do this by 'disputing' the B – the 'heat of the moment' belief sparked by any negative event. There are three ways of doing this.

Examining the evidence: What's the evidence for and/or against this belief? This is accurate thinking.

Considering the alternatives: Are there other, more optimistic explanations for what has happened? This helps develop flexible thinking.

Putting things into perspective: Is there a way of ensuring that things haven't been blown out of proportion in your mind? What action can you take to move things forward?

This process of challenging pessimistic explanations will really help to develop your optimistic 'muscle'.

Distraction

Distraction techniques can involve anything from picking up the phone to talk to a friend, to making a cup of tea, to going for a walk. Doing something different like this allows you to calm down and regroup.

Distancing

'Distancing' might mean physically removing yourself from something that is upsetting by, for example, simply stepping out of the room, or applying the distance of time and coming back to the situation at a point in the future when things feel a little less charged. This approach helps prevent you from being set back by strong negative emotions when you're in the grip of a bad experience.

In summary

In this chapter we have looked at a range of strategies that I hope will help you maintain and raise the level of your resilience to help you move through times of adversity. In the final chapter, we will bring all the knowledge together to take things to the next stage; exploring ways to facilitate post-traumatic growth itself.

CHAPTER 5

How can you grow
from adversity?

'New beginnings are often disguised as painful endings.' So said Lao Tzu, the ancient Chinese philosopher and founder of Taoism, offering a beacon of hope for anyone going through a period of adversity. The new field of post-traumatic growth shows that this is just as true in the 21st century as it was over 2,000 years ago.

While the chapters up until now have focused on coping and building resilience, the following pages are about life *after* trauma and starting to nurture the post-traumatic growth that can transform your world.

What does the journey from adversity to growth involve?

The path from adversity to growth is often not a linear one; at times something might suddenly set you back to feeling barely able to cope. Such setbacks are par for the course so try not to be discouraged when they happen and instead remember that they are a normal part of striving to overcome what life has put in your way. Trauma, grief and loss have their own rhythm and 'being positive' can feel like a tyranny. The green shoots of growth may already be present amid the suffering so try to let go of any 'shoulds' and treat yourself kindly.

The five stages of loss, according to the model put forward by psychiatrist Elisabeth Kübler-Ross in her 1969 book *On Death and Dying*, are denial, anger, bargaining, depression and acceptance. It doesn't necessarily happen in that order and the model itself has been challenged over the years, but these stages also capture something of the journey to post-traumatic growth. It's the last one (acceptance) that is key to moving on from trauma.

This was the case for the sepsis survivor we met in Chapter 2. 'My journey to recovery started with acceptance. Being told that both my legs would be amputated and that I would lose most of my fingertips was shocking news. I needed to find peace amidst this entire horrid situation. It wasn't easy and even though my illness was not my fault, accepting the situation helped me to move forward.' Accepting that life is different now is the step that opens up the gateway to what happens next.

How can you start taking active steps toward growth?

Prof. Stephen Joseph, author of *What Doesn't Kill Us*, summarizes the evidence for what people need to do to move forward from adversity as:

- Confront reality (rather than deny it)
- Accept that misfortune has happened
- Take responsibility in the aftermath for how you live your life

Below are some practices that can help facilitate the next step of turning trauma into growth:

- Constructive rumination
- Telling your story
- Adopting a 'growth mindset'

Constructive rumination

As we now know, traumatic events can shatter an individual's beliefs about the world, leading people to question their lives. Early on this 'rumination' may take the form of brooding about the causes of the distress, asking 'Why me?' or trying to figure out the crucial elements that sparked the crisis. The mind understandably gets caught up in a conflict between the old sense of self pre-trauma and the new reality post-trauma. Over time, however, the rumination can shift to become more deliberate and constructive, taking stock of life, examining the self and searching for meaning.

You can get to a sense of meaning by asking yourself if there is anything at all to take away, so to speak, from the traumatic event – the silver lining in the adversity. It may take a period of reflection before an answer eventually emerges but the bonus is that it may also lead to a new sense of purpose. I know for myself that I have made meaning from episodes of depression by putting the lessons learnt into my work as a positive psychologist. My purpose in life now is to put people on the path to happiness. Do you have a sense of purpose?

Making meaning from trauma is part of 'benefit-finding', the perception of major positive changes occurring as a result of challenging life events. As we explored in earlier chapters, these benefits include a new appreciation of your own strength and resilience, being clearer about what's really important in life, becoming more compassionate or altruistic, feeling emotionally closer to family and friends, a new openness to spiritual experience, redirected priorities or simply learning to appreciate the little things more. The outcome of benefit-finding can be significant shifts in the way we relate to the world, with reconstructed mental maps of our *inner* world altering how we are toward the *outer* world. And with an extra benefit – a sprinkling of wisdom.

Telling your story

Humans are sense-making creatures. We construct stories in the search for meaning, and to generate a new narrative when trauma takes away the picture of how we expected life to be. Trying to put the adversity into words, either to a trusted person such as a therapist or friend or by journalling about it, can be a powerful step to healing from trauma. A number of our case studies came to writing as a result of a traumatic experience (see pages 54–55 for one example).

You may already be aware of the benefits of journalling as a healing therapy – in the bestselling book *The Artist's Way* Julia Cameron recommends doing 'Morning Pages' – writing about whatever crosses your mind as a stream of consciousness. And writing a 'gratitude journal' can help you tune into and savour the positives in life.

TRYIT EXPRESSIVE WRITING

Expressive writing is a form of therapy developed by Prof. James Pennebaker at the University of Texas at Austin. People are invited to write about their trauma, what it meant to them and the feelings it generated, in 15–20 minute sessions over four consecutive days. Although people may feel upset during the process, later on they often experience an improvement in psychological well-being and physical health.

Want to give it a go? Set aside 20 minutes in a quiet place to write about any important emotional issue that is affecting you. Write by hand or on the computer and have soft music in the background if you want. As you write really let go and explore your deepest emotions and thoughts. You might mention your relationships with others; your past, present or future; who you have been or who you are now. It's up to you whether you write about the same issues each day or about different topics. Don't worry about grammar or sentence structure. The only rule is that once you begin writing, you continue until the time is up.

Based on *Pennebaker's Expressive Writing Paradigm*

Adopt a 'growth mindset'

The humanistic psychologists in the mid-20th century did much to develop the notion of 'growth'. As mentioned on pages 65–66, we humans can benefit from the 'actualizing tendency', the natural driving force within us to 'expand, develop, mature', to fulfil our potential if the right conditions are present. These include an environment that supports

CASESTUDY STEPS TO A NEW STORY

A BBC reporter on a rural cycle ride nearly died after he collided with a delivery van head-on. He was severely injured and had to spend three weeks in intensive care. Two years later he is now fully recovered but feels he has undergone significant change.

'I view life differently now. As a journalist I see news stories in a changed way, what's important and what's not have shifted. I see the human story behind a tragedy much more than I ever did. I have a greater understanding. On a wider scale I think I'm more relaxed and slightly more tolerant in life. I appreciate things for what they are and I'm more able to live in the moment. My personal views have changed too and I know small things don't matter.

genuineness (openness and self-disclosure), acceptance (being viewed with unconditional positive regard) and empathy (being listened to and understood).

Prof. Carol Dweck, a leading researcher on motivation at Stanford University, has brought a new understanding to the concept of growth. Her work has shown that there are

'I have thought often about what life means and what it is, how precious it is and how close I came to not having it. I want to try and do as much as I can, enjoy as much as I can, because this has taught me that it won't be for ever; life could end at any moment. As I recovered I was keen to look up friends who I'd begun to lose touch with. I met with several of them and that was very satisfying.

'People with head injuries often change their lives totally, and can live to regret it later. I was told about this early on and experienced it myself. I wanted to go and work for a charity, or do something I thought was worthwhile, give something back to the community. I still have a desire to do something more meaningful with my life but realize that my current job isn't without meaning or purpose. When the opportunity comes up, I'll be ready to jump.'

two types of mindset that shape our lives and these are based on the beliefs that we have about our abilities:

- The fixed mindset
- The growth mindset

Although this theory was originally geared toward understanding the ingredients of success, it also has a lot to offer when it comes to thinking about how we respond to setbacks. People with a 'fixed mindset' believe that their abilities are set in stone and not open to much development in the course of their lives. So we're all born a certain unchangeable way – smart, sporty, creative, etc. Their response to setbacks tends to be to behave in a corresponding fixed way, doing the same things over and over, feeling increasingly hopeless and helpless until they eventually give up.

Someone with a 'growth mindset', on the other hand, believes that their abilities are like plants and that with enough effort, motivation and application, they can learn, develop and grow. When they have a setback they tend to behave in a more flexible way, trying different strategies to navigate toward the goal. They don't take failure as personally as someone in a fixed mindset; they learn from things going wrong and have more self-compassion.

People in a growth mindset know the value of effort and are more likely to experiment, whereas someone with a fixed mindset is likely to be too anxious about not getting it right to allow themselves the space to try something out of their comfort zone.

The good news is that simply *knowing* about the existence of a growth mindset helps to develop one. When you're starting to rebuild your life like the phoenix rising from the ashes, making the conscious decision to adopt a growth mindset can be invaluable.

Some useful ways of doing this include:

- Being open to trying new things, for example signing up for a new course, or saying yes rather than no to unexpected invitations
- Reminding yourself of the growth mindset when you meet new challenges in life
- Aiming for progress rather than perfection
- Recognizing the power of the word 'yet', as in the affirmation 'I've not succeeded *yet*'
- Praising yourself for the effort you put in to build the motivation and resilience to continue

How can I develop the five key areas of PTG?

Remember the five dimensions that psychologists Tedeschi and Calhoun identified as being part of PTG on page 52?

- Personal strength
- Closer relationships
- Greater appreciation of life
- New possibilities
- Spiritual development

The good news is that changes in these areas are likely to happen naturally over time, but there are also some simple actions you can take to nurture them actively. Some of these have already been mentioned, but I hope you'll find it useful to consider them in direct relation to the model of transformative growth first outlined in Chapter 2.

Developing personal strength

Your greatest potential for growth comes from developing your strengths rather than focusing on fixing your weaknesses. For anyone rebuilding their life after trauma it's helpful to look to your strengths for a clue as to how to move forward in the most positive direction. They represent you at your best – your positive characteristics (personal or character strengths) and your talents (performance strengths). Finding new ways to use these character strengths has been found to increase well-

TRYIT APPLYING YOUR STRENGTHS

Recognizing and using your strengths makes it more
likely that you will excel with ease because you're
drawing on something that comes naturally to you.

You can apply your strengths like levers to reach goals:

How might your strength in _____ help you
achieve the goal of _____?

And you can also apply them to help you resolve issues:

How might your strength in _____
help you solve the problem of _____?

being and lower depression symptoms. See the box above
and also page 109 for a link to a free character strengths test.

Nurturing closer relationships

Reaching out to others is an important thing to do during
recovery from trauma; having a shoulder to lean on and
someone to support you pays dividends when you are at
your most vulnerable.

Research shows that the happiest people have good, close relationships and active social lives, which demonstrates the importance of meaningful human connection for our well-being. One very simple way to nurture relationships is to prioritize time with the people you value. For love to flourish requires a ratio of 5 to 1 positive to negative interactions according to relationship researcher John Gottman. Here are some simple ways to cultivate positive interactions with others:

- Cherish the people in your life – focus on their positives.
- Appreciate what other people do for you.
- Show empathy and compassion when others are suffering.
- Be kind to others in your everyday interactions.
- Avoid behaviours that wreck relationships, such as criticism, defensiveness, contempt and stonewalling.

Enjoying greater appreciation of life

Having your life or well-being feel threatened in some way can certainly stop you from taking it for granted. As such, gratitude is a frequent outcome of PTG. Pro-active gratitude practices include counting your blessings – such as listing three good things a day (see page 110) or writing a gratitude journal – a diary of all the positive events in your life, which you can savour whenever you need a boost. I've been keeping gratitude journals for over 20 years and it has changed my life. I went from having a scarcity mindset, aware of everything that was *missing* in my life, to a much happier abundance mindset, appreciating what I *do* have.

Searching out and embracing new possibilities
As one door closes another one does open . . . eventually. It just requires patience and the willingness to act on the

---

CASESTUDY A NEW PURPOSE IN LIFE

The mother we met on page 58 has found that, despite the hardship of having a disabled child, life has changed for the better. 'I look on this ordeal as an *awakening* – I honestly feel a newfound strength, as if I could deal with ANYTHING that life throws at me. I don't let silly, insignificant things get to me any more and if I find myself ruminating on what people have or haven't said or done, I now check myself and shrug it off.

'Going through this hardship cemented my intent to do some good, to give back to the world somehow. It inspired me to learn how to teach resilience to other carers of children with disabilities. This desire to help others – through my experience with my son – has given me a new purpose in life.'

opportunities as they arise. Being flexible and accepting that things change will help you with starting a new chapter post-trauma. How can you make the most of what there is now? How can you develop a fresh plan for each of the main areas of life such as work, home, relationships, leisure and so on? Perhaps try to identify a new set of short-, medium- and long-term goals to strive for a sense of progress.

Deepening spiritual development

Trauma can often lead people to struggle with their faith, as their beliefs are shattered and they feel let down. But when they've made peace with the trauma they may experience a deepening of faith and find themselves drawn to a *more spiritual* life. You can foster this new faith by making space for regular spiritual practice, e.g. prayer, meditation or some other form of worship. Explore the world's religions by reading their sacred texts, going on retreats or connecting with a faith community. If you prefer a more secular version of spirituality you might join a philosophy group or spend time in nature.

How do you know when you're starting to grow from adversity?

Having come through a period of crisis, at some point you may begin to recognize positive changes in yourself – such as feeling stronger or more resilient. Or you may be surprised to find an unexpected 'gift' emerging, such as a newfound sense of authenticity: you know what you really want from life now; you know who your true friends are and those you can afford to let go of.

I'd like to end this book by sharing what I consider to be one of the greatest gifts of PTG, an undervalued form of happiness that often emerges, known as 'eudaimonic well-being'. This is a concept that originated with the ancient Greek philosopher Aristotle and was about living a life of virtue, but the modern definition is something closer to flourishing and fulfilment. 'Eudaimonia' is an umbrella term describing a deeper kind of happiness, a state of psychological well-being whose elements include:

- Having a strong sense of meaning in life
- Being engaged with your life
- Making good use of your strengths
- Functioning at your best
- Serving a purpose beyond yourself
- Realizing your potential (also known as self-actualization)

A practical definition of eudaimonic well-being is that it is the experience of fulfilment that results when someone acts in accordance with their own source of meaning. It is also a form of spiritual well-being which comes about through transcendence, being motivated by something that is beyond the self. For some people this may mean a personal spiritual pathway but you may also feel you want to make a difference in the wider community, such as by:

- Pursuing a vocation or calling in life
- Helping to raise the next generation
- Supporting a community
- Contributing to a cause you're passionate about

Many people who have come through trauma feel motivated to work with others to achieve positive change in the world. It is the inspiration behind many charities – making something good come out of adversity. Having been the target of cyberstalking, what empowered me was the idea that my experience could help others. Our sepsis survivor got involved with a patient group at the hospital where his amputations were carried out. 'I've had the opportunity to talk with patients who are facing a similar situation in order to offer hope to them in what are clearly difficult times. My wife and I have also joined a choir set up to raise funds for a device to help patients who are unable to talk and communicate with staff. I was unable to talk for a week when I came out of my coma and know how difficult that is to deal with.'

So a vital personal question is: what is truly meaningful to you now that you'd be prepared to dedicate your efforts toward?

How can you perform the alchemy that can make something good out of something that was so painful? What ripple can you send out into the world as a positive legacy from the traumatic events you have lived through?

One of the benefits of eudaimonic well-being is that it is longer-lasting and more sustainable than the short-term happiness of hedonic well-being, which comes from the pursuit of pleasure.

And finally

Together we have been on a journey through adversity and now we have come out the other end in a place of growth. Whether you've just experienced a trauma yourself, think someone close to you might be experiencing PTS or are starting to feel more resilient after a period of feeling lost and overwhelmed, learning about the phenomenon of PTG can be a turning point.

I hope that this book has been a source of comfort for you, helping to guide you through to recovery and increasing your chances of finding ways to transform trauma into growth. As one of the people in the case studies puts it, 'I wouldn't change what happened or my life for the world; this experience has made me a stronger person and happy in my own shoes.'

What next?

I have a coaster on my desk that reads 'Where there's tea, there's hope.' A cup of tea has certainly sustained me through many a difficult moment as well as through the writing of this book. My hope is that learning about post-traumatic growth will be a game-changer for you, assuring you that things *can* change, that there is light at the end of the tunnel, and that there is reason to be hopeful about the possibilities for the future.

To this end I have suggested some further reading and useful websites in the following pages, which will allow you to explore PTG further.

'Look on the bright side' is a piece of advice that is often dished out but will sound hollow and somewhat alien to anyone who is going through adversity. While there is no doubt that optimism has significant benefits for your psychological and physical well-being, understandably it can be difficult to think optimistically when your life is in pieces. That's why I like the scientific conceptualization of hope, something that post-traumatic growth can offer you when you're ready – a practical pathway to positive change.

One approach to hope that I find helpful is breaking it down into three practical steps, so when you're ready you might like to try the following:

- Identify what you would ideally like in life (the goal)
- Think of a variety of routes toward this goal (pathways)
- Apply yourself with motivation and energy along these pathways to achieve the goal (agency)

Taking action like this is fundamental in moving forward after trauma. I know from my years of experience in the field of positive psychology that there is only so far you can get with *reading* about the subject. The change will only ever come with putting the knowledge into *action*. Happiness is not a spectator sport; it is the practice of techniques like the ones outlined in this book that forms the neural pathways to make a habit out of happiness. My hope is that the content of this book will give you hope that you are not alone, inspiration that you will get through tough times, and knowledge and tools to help you rebuild your life from the inside out. Where there is a will there will almost certainly be a way.

Further reading

I recommend these books to continue your exploration of the journey from PTS to PTG.

Akhtar, Miriam, *Positive Psychology for Overcoming Depression*, Watkins, 2012

Bannink, Fredrike, *Post Traumatic Success*, Norton, 2014

Boniwell, Ilona, *Positive Psychology in a Nutshell*, PWBC, 2006

Calhoun, Lawrence, and Richard Tedeschi, *Posttraumatic Growth in Clinical Practice*, Routledge, 2013

Craig, Gary, *EFT for PTSD*, Energy Psychology Press, 2009

Dweck, Carol, *Mindset: How You Can Fulfil Your Potential*, Random House, 2006

Frankl, Viktor, *Man's Search for Meaning*, Beacon Press, 2006

Fredrickson, Barbara, *Positivity*, Crown, 2009

Gottman, John, and Nan Silver, *The Seven Principles for Making Marriage Work*, Three Rivers Press, 1999

Hefferon, Kate, and Ilona Boniwell, *Positive Psychology: Theory, Research and Applications*, Open University, 2011

Johnstone, Chris, *Find Your Power: A Toolkit for Resilience and Positive Change*, 2nd edn, Permanent Publications, 2010

Ivtzan, Itai, Tim Lomas, Kate Hefferon, Piers Worth, *Second Wave Positive Psychology*, Routledge, 2016

Joseph, Stephen, *What Doesn't Kill Us*, Piatkus, 2011

Lal, Tara, *Standing on my Brother's Shoulders*, Watkins, 2015

Reivich, Karen, and Andrew Shatté, *The Resilience Factor*, Broadway Books, 2003

Rendon, Jim, *Upside*, Touchstone Press, 2015

Rothschild, Babette, *The Body Remembers: The Psychophysiology of Trauma and Trauma Treatment*, Norton, 2000

Seligman, Martin, *Learned Optimism*, Alfred A Knopf, 1990

Seligman, Martin, *Flourish*, Nicholas Brealey Publishing, 2011

Shapiro, Francine, *Getting Past Your Past: Take Control of Your Life with Self-Help Techniques from EMDR Therapy*, Rodale, 2013

van der Kolk, Bessel, *The Body Keeps the Score*, Penguin, 2015

Ware, Bronnie, *The Top 5 Regrets of the Dying*, Hay House UK, 2012

Williams, Mark, John Teasdale, Zindel Segal, Jon Kabat-Zinn, *The Mindful Way Through Depression*, Guilford Press, 2007

Useful websites

The major research bodies studying PTG include the following:

The Post Traumatic Growth Research Unit at the University of East London:
> www.uel.ac.uk/Schools/Psychology/Research/Health-Promotion-and-Behaviour/Post-Traumatic-Growth

The PTG research group at the University of North Carolina where Tedeschi and Calhoun, the originators of PTG, are based:
> https://ptgi.uncc.edu

The Centre for Trauma, Resilience and Growth:
> www.nottinghamshirehealthcare.nhs.uk/centre-for-trauma-resilience-growth

Other useful websites providing a variety of resources and additional information are:

University of Pennsylvania's positive psychology website:
> www.authentichappiness.sas.upenn.edu

Penny Brohn UK. Living well with cancer: www.pennybrohn.org.uk

MIND: www.mind.org.uk

HelpGuide: www.helpguide.org

Web-MD: www.webmd.com

Diagnostic and Statistical Manual, 5th edition: www.dsm5.org

National Center for PTSD: www.ptsd.va.gov

PTSD UK: www.ptsduk.org

Black Dog Institute: www.blackdoginstitute.org.au

Green Exercise Research Group, University of Essex:
> www.greenexercise.org